Listen to This:

More Mostly True Stories Worth the Tellin'

Suellen Alfred and Joyce Milligan Tatum

Listen to This: More Mostly True Stories Worth the Tellin'
ISBN: Softcover 978-1-946478-34-4

To order additional copies of this book, contact:

Parson's Porch Books
1-423-475-7308
www.parsonsporch.com

Parson's Porch Books is an imprint of **Parson's Porch & Book Publishers** in Cleveland, Tennessee, which has double focus. We focus on the needs of creative writers who need a professional publisher to get their work to market, **&** we also focus on the needs of others by sharing our profits with those who struggle in poverty to meet their basic needs of food, clothing, shelter and safety.

Listen to This

Dedication

From Joyce: To my children Tiffany, Jennifer, and Jeremy. I love you all dearly.

From Suellen: In memory of my dear aunt Blanche Murray Nunnelley and my mother Freeda Murray Alfred. The joy of their stories rocked the house with laughter.

From Joyce and Suellen: To all the people who have taken the time to read and to listen to our stories with smiling faces and positive comments. Without listeners, storytellers would have nowhere to go.

A Word of Thanks

We are grateful to our dear friend, eagle eye Jere Mitchum, who was very helpful with his copy editing of the manuscript. If there are any mistakes in this book, they are not his but ours alone.

Contents

Introduction

When we hear "Listen to this," most of us are all ears. It is a good way to capture the attention of folks to whom we want to tell a story. That phrase holds the promise of hearing something interesting, or informative, or funny. As for the words "mostly true" as a part of the book's title, we suspect that is the case with every story that is told. On the question of truth, the words of Susan Estrich ring true: "... truth is a construct, infected with the biases of the teller."[1] A story, true or not, comes from a particular point of view from a teller who may concentrate on parts of the story that another teller might leave out. As Bryce Stevens has said, "In the telling, we discover ourselves. And in the listening, we learn that none of us is alone." We hope that will be the case for the people who read this book and hear our stories.

---

1 Susan Estrich. "Who Cares About the Distractions?" *Herald Citizen*. Cookeville, TN, May 4, 2017, p. 4.

The Christmas Tree That Would Not Stand

By Pam Petty

(If you still believe in the magic and wonder of tree-trimming, gift-buying, holiday-meal-fixing, and harmonious family gatherings, you probably don't want to read this. For those of you like me, who are also strung-out, spent-out, smiled-out, and ho-hoed out, read along.)

For twenty-two years of marriage, my husband and I have always had a live Christmas tree. Sometimes it is a cut tree, sometimes it is a tree that can be replanted, but never is it an artificial tree. So, each year requires the ritual of procuring the new live tree. This almost never happens without incident. Some of the stories can be told now because enough time has passed that the pain has somewhat eased. But it may be years and years before any of us can tell the story of last year's tree without pointing fingers (could be any one of a variety of fingers) or breaking down.

For the first time in our Christmas-tree-buying history, we were able to go to a local Christmas tree farm and, as a family, select, cut, and gleefully bring our own Christmas tree over the threshold into our home. My husband, our two teenage children, and I piled into the pickup truck and drove to the Christmas Tree Farm. I had visions of the Waltons chopping down their own tree and gleefully bringing it across the threshold of their happy home. When we got to the farm, we walked from tree to tree. Each time we found a tree that we liked, my husband lay down on the ground and looked from the bottom of the tree to the top to see if the tree was straight. After doing this about 14 times, each time he pronounced that the tree was crooked. It was apparent to me that there were no straight trees. I figured we might as well buy the prettiest crooked tree we could find. (Stereotypical "female" logic I have since been told.) Everyone was getting pretty tired out from all this tree shopping. The kids were whining, my husband was covered with pine needles, and the "glow" of this whole process had worn off. We finally purchased the prettiest crooked tree we could find and loaded it in the back of the truck for the short ride home.

I now know how the people in "Poltergeist" felt with an evil presence in the house! We pulled out our trusty tree stand, the one that has held many beautiful trees over the years. I held the tree as my husband tightened the screws that are supposed to hold the tree at the base in place. Two hours later, bathed in sweat, my eyes puffy from my allergy to pine trees, and many verbal exchanges later (the likes of which cannot be printed here), my husband and I threw the tree stand away. Casualty number one.

Thinking that the tree stand was old and that a new tree stand would be stronger, we began our quest for an industrial strength tree stand. All the while the new tree was lying on its side in the den, looking like a fallen soldier - dying of thirst. Hunter that he is, my husband came home with another tree stand that had required a trip to Wal-Mart and one to the hardware store. We would prevail. Monday night we began again with me holding the tree upright and my husband tightening the new super-strength screws. We twisted, we turned, we discussed physics and who in our household was not living right. We finally got the tree to stand erect, quickly put on the lights and went to bed satisfied with ourselves. The next morning, we entered the den to find the tree on its side and forever looking like cats had been running in circles through it. We threw away the new, twisted, pathetic tree stand, and propped the tree up in the corner leaving sappy smears on the walls. Casualty number two.

I don't know if we are simply a determined group of people or if we are just stupid, but the next day my husband drove to Lebanon, Tennessee, and bought another tree stand that exemplified the latest in tree-stand technology. We spent yet another evening in an attempt to have a vertical Christmas tree. I can't tell you the complete sequence of events because my mind is cloudy on the details, but I can tell you that saws, wires, nails, and lawyers were discussed during the course of the evening. For about 40 minutes, just long enough for us to re-string the lights on the tree, it stood erect and then slowly started going south. It was clear that my husband and I could no longer work together on this project. During the course of that evening, after repeated attempts to straighten it, the tree got shorter (thanks to the saw); recounts of how this Christmas tree came into our possession no longer resembled reality; and yet another Christmas tree stand died a cruel death. Casualty number three.

Fearing that casualty number four would defeat my husband or me, I took matters into my own hands. The next morning as I saw yet another pool of water spilled from the dilapidated tree stand, broken ornaments, and twisted lights, I began fantasizing about draining the gas from the John Deere and having myself a little "tree lighting" ceremony. I was looking for a siphon of some sort when I found the saw. Figuring that a little saw dust on my floor couldn't make matters much worse, I began my attack on the lower limbs of that tree. Several limbs and a couple of wrestling matches later, our forever shrinking tree lay waiting for my next attack. I went to the garage and brought in this huge black, plastic bucket. With a sudden burst of super-human strength, I grabbed that tree by the trunk and shoved it down into the bucket. The base of the trunk did not reach the bottom, but I balanced the tree on its branches across the top of the bucket. I can only imagine the wild look in my eyes at this point, for there was no one here to witness this spectacle and, therefore, no one except me who has to live with the memories.

Refusing to take the decorations off the tree and start all over, I did a "patch" job on the askew ornaments and twisted lights. I added gallons of water to the bucket and plugged in the lights, fully aware that I would probably be electrocuted and the tree would be the winner after all. Much to my surprise, the lights worked (at least most of them; I was not picky at this point). The final touch was to add the beautiful, old-world Santa, all dressed in cream-colored, fur-trimmed velvet, to the top of the tree. The branches at the top of the tree were twisted and frayed from the previous days' abuse, and I had to cram a whole handful of the top of the tree into the Santa to get him to stay up there. The final effect was that Santa was slightly tilted to the east and was looking heavenward. It looked like he was praying. I suspect those prayers were the result of my exclamation that if the tree fell again, the tree, every ornament, light and tree-topper (namely, Santa) will be thrown in the river behind our house.

On day five of operation "Tree Stands Alone" I was able to walk through the room without flinching when I saw the tree. My family knew not to mention the tree to me. By the back door, I put up a sign that read, "THANK YOU FOR NOT MENTIONING THE CHRISTMAS TREE," warning any unsuspecting, holiday-spirit-filled people who might walk into my house and innocently proclaim, "Oh, what a beautiful tree!" I simply did not want to hear it.

A Christmas Memory

By Heidemarie Z. Weidner

My father prided himself on saving money at all times and in all situations. His ambition to make a good deal included even the purchase of a Christmas tree. Every year he would come home and brag that he had been able to buy the most beautiful tree at the best price. Of course, those "most beautiful" trees had to undergo several delicate operations to achieve perfection, and my father seemed to enjoy those adjustments as much as he did his wheeling and dealing. Several cuts with a saw balanced a tree's crooked height, and skillful drilling allowed my father to move branches according to his vision of symmetry. If all his labors failed to recreate the perfect Christmas tree, he invariably would say, "Oh, well. Once it is decorated, you won't be able to see a thing." He believed that candles, ornaments, and glitter would hide all blemishes. And, of course, my father was always right. At least as far as Christmas trees were concerned.

One year my father came up with the idea that a free tree would be best of all. I don't remember how old I was then, but I must have been still young enough that the plan of stealing a Christmas tree could excite me. I am a bit ashamed of telling on my father now; at the same time, this story shows a side of him that I have always found endearing: his boyishness and enjoyment of pranks. Even in his sixties he could still pretend to his grandchildren that he was about to lose his balance in the boat they shared, and then actually lose it and fall, with a great splash, into the murky waters of our lake. To their—and his—delight!

The night before we set out to steal the tree it snowed, turning our village and its surroundings into an expanse of whiteness, here and there intersected with clusters of wind-bent trees and small copses of wood.

"I know a place behind the Rose Garden (all fields and woods in our region of southern Germany had wonderful, evocative names) with a small planting of young firs," my father confided in me as we trudged through the fresh snow. We were dressed warmly to protect against the bitter wind that swept off the high plains into the valley. My father carried a large brown burlap sack on his shoulders. It hid the axe he needed to cut the tree. In my mind, I picture our dark figures against the brilliant white of the snow as we were walking the New Road towards the valley, then veering a sharp right to cross the pastures of the Lähle[2], and finally turning into the lane along the hedges of the Rose Garden where in late fall we children had gathered the small hips of roses to make tea and preserves. Behind us stayed the cluster of old farmhouses with smoke drifting from their chimneys in the early morning air. A painting of Brueghel.

On the other side of the Rose Garden, the ground sloped toward the river Jagst valley and civilization with the two-story school house, the church of St. Mary, and the small castle dating back to the 14th century. In front of us, a small clearing had been planted with fir trees. They stood thick and dark and silent. Our talk quieted, too. Even the wind had subsided. All we could hear was our labored breathing. Carefully my father approached the trees, glancing furtively around every so often.

All of a sudden, a sound out of nowhere! My father threw himself down between the rows of trees and motioned to me. I followed his example. He put his finger to his lips. With my heart pounding, I lay utterly still. The snow felt soft and cold, and yellow grasses poked my face. I felt afraid and safe at the same time. Snow. A dark grove of trees. Silence. And my father and me. What more could a child want?

When we finally got up, we felt like comrades in arms. "A rabbit or a deer," my father shrugged off my question—a bit sheepishly, I thought—while brushing off the snow from his clothes. We cut the perfect tree and carried it home to tell our story.

Today, as I am writing about it for the first time, I wonder: Was my father really afraid? Or did he just want to give us both a marvelous adventure?

---

[2] Sorry, my translator's skill just left me.

The Angel of the Lord

By Sid Gilbreath

(Sid Gilbreath wants to thank Jennie Ivey for encouraging him to submit this story to the *Herald-Citizen* where it originally appeared in the December 20, 2015 issue.)

"Drat!" I muttered, smacking the palms of my hands a little too hard against the steering wheel of my 1952 Ford. Dusk was falling fast on Knoxville, Tennessee; and though I'd traveled almost the entire length of Main Street, I still hadn't found a filling station that was open on Christmas Eve. This was a problem, for sure, because I was supposed to drive my new bride, Pat, and her widowed mother to a big family celebration in a neighboring town the next morning. Wanting to impress these new relatives, many of whom I hadn't yet met, I'd spent hours washing and polishing my five-year-old olive green coupe until it shone. All for naught, unless I could find some gas to put in the tank.

Just as I was about to give up hope, I spotted a station with its neon sign still glowing. And there stood a snappily-dressed attendant, white cap and all, ready to pump gas, check the oil, and clean my windshield. Hallelujah! I would soon be headed home.

Directly ahead of me on the nearly deserted street was a bus. It slowed as it approached a woman and a little boy who were waving anxiously from the curb. But the bus driver didn't stop. Instead he turned the corner and sped out of sight. When the smoke from his exhaust cleared, I saw why.

The woman and the child were black. Any Southerner can tell you that before the Civil Rights Acts of the 1960's, discrimination like that was common.

Absorbed in my own thoughts, most of which centered on a mouth-watering Christmas Eve supper of pot roast and carrots and potatoes in a room with a yet-to-be-decorated cedar tree. I almost drove on, too. But somehow, I just couldn't. The twosome looked too sad and desperate. So, I pulled to the curb and leaned over to crank down the passenger-side window.

"Hello," I said. "Is there some way I can help you?"

Though dressed in coats and hats, the two lonely figures were shivering in the frigid December air. The little boy, who looked to be about seven years old, wiped away tears with the back of his hand. "Two buses passed us by," the woman said, the shyness in her voice mixed with anger and frustration. "My son Michael here," she gently squeezed the boy's shoulder as she spoke, "is supposed to play the Angel of the Lord in our church Christmas pageant tonight. " She pushed up her coat sleeve and glanced at her watch. "It starts in less than an hour. And I don't know when another bus will be by. . " Unspoken but hanging in the air was the end of the sentence: "or if it will stop."

I thought about Pat, eagerly awaiting my return to our tiny basement apartment for our first Christmas Eve together as husband and wife. I had no way to call her. In 1957, only Dick Tracy had a cell phone. Looking for a pay phone would waste precious time. So, I did the only thing I could do. I whispered a little prayer that Pat wouldn't worry and that these persons of a race different than mine – a seemingly insurmountable difference in the 1950's American South – would accept the offer I was about to make.

I pushed the passenger door open. "Climb in," I said. "I'll drive you to church."

Michael clambered into the back seat. His mother started to follow. "No need for that," I said softly. "You are more than welcome to sit up front."

She offered me a little smile. "I'm Mrs. Johnson," she said. She told me the address of her church which was a half-hour drive away. "Now, if you don't mind," she said, "I need to help Michael go over his lines before we get there."

While I drove and fretted about Pat, Michael's mother twisted around toward the back seat. "Fear not." she began.

"For behold, "Michael chimed in, "I bring you good tidings of great joy which. which.

"Shall be." his mother whispered.

"Which shall be to all people." I could hear the joy in Michael's small voice as he completed the sentence.

"Now," she said, "say it all at once. Slowly and loudly, so that the folks in the back row at church can hear."

Michael repeated his lines flawlessly.

"Now the next part," his mother said. "For unto you is born."

"Jesus, the Lord!"

Mrs. Johnson and I looked at each other and grinned.

"That's the right idea, Michael," she said. "But you need to say it just like the Bible does. For unto you is born this day in the city of David a Savior."

"Who is Christ the Lord."

I waved one fist in the air. "That a boy, Michael."

"Now for the last part," Mrs. Johnson said. "And this shall be a sign unto you."

Michael finished, ". Ye shall find the babe wrapped in swaddling clothes, lying in a manger."

My heart felt ready to burst. For the rest of the ride, Michael practiced his lines repeatedly. By the time, we pulled into the church parking lot, he was saying them without one bit of prompting. Tears welled up in Mrs. Johnson's eyes as she reached for the door handle of the car. "Thank you from the bottom of my heart," she said. "We'd be honored to have you join us for the service."

I shook my head. "I'd love to. But my wife and mother-in-law are waiting for me at home with what I'm certain is a very overdone pot roast."

Mrs. Johnson reached into her purse and pulled out a wad of money. "I want to pay for your gas," she said. "And for your time and trouble."

Again, I shook my head. "It was no trouble. And you've already paid me. Sharing Christmas Eve with you and Michael is a gift I'll never forget."

I watched as Mrs. Johnson helped the Angel of the Lord out of the backseat. Michael took her hand and then looked back at me and waved as I pulled out of the parking lot.

More than sixty years have passed since that cold December night. Pat and I still talk and laugh about how worried and – yes – just a wee bit angry she was when I didn't show up in time for dinner. But that conversation never fails to remind me that, like the innkeeper in Bethlehem 2000 years ago, I was blessed to be given the chance to help a frightened mother and her son bring good tidings of great joy to our little corner of the world.

It was a Christmas Eve to remember always.

All the Privacy You Want: Andrew Jackson and the Innkeeper

By Suellen Alfred

(This account is based on a story found in LaReine Warden Clayton, *Stories of Early Inns and Taverns of the East Tennessee Country*. Nashville: National Society of Colonial Dames of America in the State of Tennessee, 1995, p. 55.)

One night during the early nineteenth century, Amis Inn in Rogersville, Tennessee, was full. All rooms were taken. A stranger came in with a sour look on his face. He walked up to Mary Amis, the owner, and leaned toward her in a menacing manner. "I want a private room," he said gruffly.

Mary was a little intimidated by this very rude ruffian, but she had no choice but to turn him down.

"I'm sorry, sir, but we have no private rooms left. They are all taken," said Mary.

"Surely to God you have a private room set aside for someone who wants to have one."

"No sir. We have no private rooms left. If you want to stay here, you will have to share a room with another guest who has already reserved it."

"I said I want a private room in this inn, and I am not leaving until I have one," said the man.

"Well, unless you are willing to share a room with another man, I suppose you will stand right there for a few uncomfortable days," she said.

"How dare you talk to me that way, young woman! Why, I ought to give you a spanking right here."

Unfortunately for him, the man did not realize that Andrew Jackson, the future President of the United States, was also in the parlor. Andrew Jackson was not a man to mess with. Now most people know that Andrew Jackson had a reputation for losing his temper. Mary Amis was a friend of Jackson's; and he did not like the conversation he was hearing at all. When the man said he was going to stay there until he got a private room, Jackson had heard enough.

"I'll give him a private room," Jackson said.

He took the man by the arm, and ushered him out of the room through the yard to the log corncrib in the rear of the premises. Shoving the reluctant visitor into the corncrib, Jackson bolted the door and locked him in.

"Now, sir," Jackson said. "In there you'll have all the privacy you want. " He marched back to the inn, and had a very pleasant visit with his friend Mary Amis.

No one knows how long the man stayed in his "private room" before some sympathetic soul let him out to go on his way.

The Best Job in the World

By Megan Trotter

(This story first appeared in the *Herald Citizen*, Sunday, July 5, 2009 where Megan Trotter is a staff writer in Cookeville, Tennessee.)

As a writer for the Cookeville *Herald Citizen,* I have one of the best jobs in the world. Not only do I get to write, which I love, but I also get to learn about the amazing things that other people do. I recently interviewed Kristen Bobo, a Cookeville caver who is featured in a recent issue of the *National Geographic Magazine.* Toward the end of our interview, I said, in a sort-of offhanded way, that I'd love to explore a cave someday.

"What about next week?" Kristen asked. "I could take you next weekend."

I spent the next week and a half being ridiculously excited.

When the big weekend finally rolled around, I found myself sitting in the back of Kristen's vehicle with my 19-year-old sister, Emily, and Kristen's boyfriend and archeologist, Bill. While we enjoyed the pleasant drive, Kristen explained how the caves were made while Bill told how Native Americans would explore these caves barefoot with nothing to light their way except a few torches. I was glad we would have electric lights on our helmets when we went inside.

When we finally arrived at a cave in White County, Kristen unlocked the gate; and we descended a ladder into chilly darkness. As soon as my feet touched the ground, my sneakers sank into mud. It took me only a few seconds to regret not spending some money on proper boots. Within the first few minutes of our trip, my shoes felt like they weighed ten pounds each. I soon forgot about the mud, though, as my head lamp made strange and beautiful rock formations materialize out of the blackness surrounding us.

There were small, delicate formations that looked like someone had stuck a handful of straws underneath the outcropping of rock, and large, wavy formations that looked like pieces of bacon balancing on their edges. One large grouping of these bacon formations looked almost like some enormous prehistoric butterfly. As beautiful as they were, these formations, Kristen informed us, were "dead." When a hole was blasted in the side of the mountain to make easier access for medical personnel to get to anyone injured in the cave, the air had dried out the formations close to this new hole and guaranteed that they would not grow any larger.

Deeper inside the cave was a different story. There were columns of living rock growing straight up out of the ground. Great wavy curtains of rock hung from the ceiling, some growing downward long enough to touch the stalagmites growing underneath them. Some of my favorites were the giant honeycomb-shaped formations that held shallow pools of water. The inside edges of the exposed "honeycomb" glittered as if they were encrusted with diamonds.

The most difficult part of our excursion, at least in my mind, was what I like to refer to as the Crawl of Claustrophobia. During one of our breaks, Kristen mentioned that up ahead was a spot where, in order to get through, we would have to get down on our hands and knees and crawl a bit. I nodded absentmindedly while taking a swig of water from my canteen. That didn't sound so bad. I could handle that. Then after that, Kristen said that we'd have to get down, not on hands and knees but on our *stomachs* and crawl for a little way. That I wasn't so OK with.

When we arrived at the spot Kristen had described, my uneasiness only increased. What she wanted us to crawl under was a massive ceiling of solid rock. Without hesitation Kristen got down on her stomach and started wiggling through the passage. I watched, still unsure if I would be able to follow, as she crawled along what seemed like a fairly short distance before disappearing through a crevice. She called back to us to tell us she was standing in a large cavern.

Because the crevice where I could see Kristen's light shining through did not seem all that far away, I decided to attempt the crawl. After all, when would I ever get this opportunity again? After checking with my sister to make sure she thought she could attempt it, too, I took a deep breath, dropped down to my stomach and followed Kristen's previous path. I tried not to think about my helmet knocking on the rock overhead and instead focused on just pulling myself through as quickly as possible.

We all made it through without incident, and I was thrilled to hear that no more "claustrophobia crawls" would be required. After about two hours and three-fourths of a mile from the time we entered the cave, we reached our final destination, the Cathedral Room. The enormous cavern was filled with spectacular formations that glittered in our dim helmet lights. From the top of the ceiling that was so high it dissolved into darkness, all the way down to the rocky floor, formations in various shades of white and red covered almost every inch. It looked as if someone had lit a giant candle and let the wax just roll down the sides of the cave. We stayed in that cavern for a long while, resting from our journey, snapping pictures and just enjoying the breathtaking beauty.

When we finally decided it was time to head back, the return trip was relatively uneventful except in one cavern where we had to wade through icy, shin-deep water. I had been following behind Kristen, slightly annoyed at getting wet again after I had just dried off from our first trip through the water, when I took a step and suddenly found no ground underneath my right foot. I was thigh-deep in ice water before I caught myself on a nearby cave formation. I'm not sure how deep the hole actually was, as my foot never touched the bottom, but I had visions of an ancient water-dwelling cave creature eyeing my leg for dinner. I quickly jerked my leg up out of the hole and onto dry land with all of my body parts intact and only a tender spot on my shin that I had knocked against the edge of the bottomless pit when I fell. I also regretted not buying shin guards.

On the drive back into town, I could really tell that Kristen and Bill were more experienced cavers than my sister and me. As they chatted about our latest adventure all the way back into town, my sister and I more or less passed out in the back seat. Before we got into the vehicles, though, Bill turned to me and chuckled, "This was a lot of trouble for you to go through for a story."

Not at all, I thought as I collapsed on the ground and tried to wiggle out of my filthy kneepads. This is one of the best jobs in the world.

How's Your Mama?

By Joyce Milligan Tatum

In our neck of the woods, upon seeing an acquaintance after an absence of a day or two, it is a common practice to ask about that person's family. We are so eager to hear the latest family news that our curiosity sometimes overcomes our good manners, and we may ask a question that some people prefer not to answer. This habit is uniquely embarrassing when we ask those questions in a public place such as a restaurant or in church.

"Has your sister gotten a date for the dance? Poor thing. Was your daddy able to get that bail money together to get your brother out of jail again?" These questions are really not rude to us. They are a sign of endearment, of concern and affection. The older a person is, the more likely she or he is to ask some embarrassing questions that a younger person feels should be left unsaid.

My husband Alan and I had stopped for lunch at a family-owned restaurant one Sunday at noon. We were seated at a table next to a large group of people from at least three generations. The oldest member of the group whom they called Miss Claire appeared to be in her early seventies. She knew everyone, and everyone knew her. As people entered the main dining room, she called out to them in a very loud voice.

"Helen. Helen, honey, how are you doing? Did you make it to church this morning? I went to the early service myself because Brother Frank preaches at that service and he doesn't have much time, so it's a shorter service. I like that." Helen spoke to Miss Claire and moved on.

Soon the restaurant had reached a comfortably full number of diners, when in came Vernell and her family. Miss Claire greeted her very loudly, "Vernell! Vernell! Oh, honey how's your mama? I have been praying for her hemorrhoids all week!"

Now the restaurant got quiet very quickly. Several gentlemen bowed their heads with smirks on their faces, and several ladies raised their napkins to their mouths. Vernell's face immediately reddened. "She's fine, Miss Claire. Just fine," she said and hurried away toward a table at the opposite end of the restaurant. But Miss Claire wasn't finished. In a loud voice for all to hear she said, "You tell her that I'm going to keep praying for those hemorrhoids to just shrink up. Oh, how painful those things are." No one dared have eye contact with Miss Clair for fear that she would loudly share his or her family's ailments as well. Miss Clair continued to call attention the health of many people in the restaurant. Nothing like having a whole restaurant full of people knowing about your mama's delicate health.

By this time even her family members were trying to hush Miss Claire. One of her sons called for the check, and her daughter remarked on how late it was getting and that they should be getting on toward the house. Miss Claire, still smiling, got up and went to several tables to speak to the patrons there. Few of them gave her eye contact, and no one greeted her with any enthusiasm. They were all mightily relieved when Miss Claire's daughter gently touched her on the shoulder and said, "Mama, it's time to leave." Her son paid the bill and rushed over to "help" Miss Claire toward the door.

As soon as she was gone, everyone in the restaurant burst into laughter with such remarks as "Lord love her," and "Miss Claire's on a roll today." Probably the most meaningful remark came from someone who was familiar with Miss Claire's health: "They need to increase her medication

You's A Killin' My Mama

By Joyce Milligan Tatum

Sometimes in my daily duties at the pharmacy I am called upon to make deliveries. I enjoy this job; and, because I never deliver any of the hard drugs, I feel safe. It gets me out of the building, and I get to meet some of the most interesting people.

On one particular day, a prescription was called in for an elderly lady who lived with her daughter out in the country. I mean way out in the country! You know you might be in trouble when the GPS in your car has no clue where you are or where you are going. In fact, on more than one occasion, the turn-by-turn voice navigation system very firmly but erroneously told me to "MAKE A U-TURN, NOW! I did not do so. I followed the daughter's directions and finally reached my destination.

It was an older single-wide mobile home that had been well cared for, but was very dated.

Gold colored shag carpet covered the entrance area and the living room to my right as I came through the door. To my left was a kitchen with avocado colored appliances and a linoleum floor.

The daughter opened the door for me and greeted me with a very southern, country, backwoods drawl. Her mother, our client, was sitting at the table eating in the dimly lit dining area. She nodded to me as I entered.

"How ye doin'?" the daughter asked. "C'mon in. I knowed you was a comin', and I was lookin' fer ye."

I introduced myself and began to explain how to use the medicine I had brought for her mother. Suddenly the elderly lady began to gasp and wheeze, as if she could not catch her breath. Both the daughter and I looked over at her with some concern.

"You's a killin' my mama," the daughter said.

I blinked a few times and tried to absorb what she had said. Again, the elderly lady gasped and jerked. Dumbfounded, I looked at the daughter.

"You's a killin' my mama," she said again, with no explanation.

"What? I don't. I." I didn't know what to say.

The daughter looked at me, stomped her foot and said, "You's a standin' on her *auxagen* cord!"

That's when I realized her mother was wearing a clear nasal oxygen cord that ran from her nose to the oxygen tank in the corner of the living room. The cord ran some fourteen feet through the shag carpet. I simply had not seen it.

I jumped and began to apologize profusely to both the daughter and the mother. The daughter hurried over to her mother and said, "It's all right, Mama. She didn't mean to try to kill ye."

I left in a hurry.

When I got back to the pharmacy, I called the home health nurse who had been assigned to the elderly lady. I explained tearfully what I had done, hoping I had not harmed the woman.

The nurse began to laugh and said to me, "Don't worry about it. I did the same thing to her last week."

Mama 'Cile's Driving

By Joyce Milligan Tatum

My husband's grandmother, Lucille, lost her beloved husband, Roy, in 1967, after fifty years of marriage. Mama 'Cile, as we called her, had never learned to drive. Daddy Roy took her everywhere she wanted to go. Several months after his passing, she decided she needed to learn to drive. She began each day by going out to the car and simply sitting in the driver's seat until she felt comfortable with it. She found the owner's manual for the car and studied it for a week. She learned about the windshield wipers, headlights, door locks, and tire pressure. She learned how to raise the hood and how to change the oil. At age seventy-three she coerced various people in town to teach her how to put her "book learning" into practice. Some brave souls had the courage to ride with her as she practiced her driving, causing near panic among the citizens of the small town of Kenton.

She went to the eye doctor for new glasses, located her birth certificate, and went to the driver's testing center where she obtained a copy of the state driving license handbook and read it a few times. After a few weeks of studying the handbook and practicing her driving, she appeared at the Highway Patrol office in Union City, Tennessee to take the test. No one was surprised when she passed the written test, but how she passed the driving test is anyone's guess. Maybe she had to drive around the block making right turns only, or maybe the officer felt sorry for her. Perhaps he just wanted to get rid of her, since we were sure that as she drove around the appointed driving test route, she told him her life story, as she did with anyone who would listen; or maybe he mistakenly marked the box by the word "pass" when he should have marked the box by the word "fail." Who knows? For whatever reason, she got her driver's license.

Thank goodness Kenton, Tennessee is a small town. When Mama 'Cile was on the road, for some reason she had it in her mind that the center line was what you straddled to keep you from going off in the ditch on either side of the road. People who lived in the area quickly learned that if that 1962 beige Chevrolet Impala was on the road, you needed to swerve to the shoulder and get out of the way. Unaware strangers were on their own.

She never drove fast. Fifteen to twenty miles an hour was speeding to her. She never got the hang of parking. She generally parked head first in a parking lot by the building she intended to enter. She simply came to a stop when she hit the building. She did know her limitations. She only drove to six places – the post office, the grocery store, the beauty shop, the doctor's office, church, and her daughter's house. Folks who were en route to or from those locations quickly learned to move over as far as they could to accommodate Mama 'Cile's driving.

Mama 'Cile's daughter, Anne, lived in the country about three miles from Mama 'Cile. When Anne and her family moved back to Kenton from Chicago, Mama 'Cile was overjoyed. She would have six grandchildren nearby to love and spoil. As the grandchildren got older and married, she saw her brood getting larger and larger, and she loved it. I was very happy to add to that number of grandchildren. Three years after Alan and I married, I became pregnant. When we informed Mama 'Cile that she was going to be a great-grandmother, she was overjoyed.

One Saturday Alan and I were at her house where she was showing me all the things she had bought for our new baby. Alan wanted to go on to his mother's house so he could watch a football game with his brothers. Mama 'Cile told him to go on. She would drive me over after the lemon cake she had in the oven was ready. Before I could protest, he kissed the top of my head and took off out her front door. I felt a little uneasy, but then I realized I could drive us there in Mama 'Cile's car.

Thirty minutes later we were ready to go as Mama 'Cile proudly took up her cake in a cake carrier and headed toward the door. I picked up the car keys and told Mama 'Cile I would drive. She snatched them from me quickly and informed me that in my condition, I had no business driving. I followed her out the door and obediently got in the car.

Less than a mile from Anne's house we came to a mile-long stretch of road that is straight and narrow. As we reached that section, I could see a very large tractor pulling a very large plow coming toward us. I knew it was Mr. Earl, since no one else in the area had a tractor or plow that big.

Sure enough, Mama 'Cile was straddling that yellow line right in the middle of the road. She usually got away with it because everyone in town simply moved over when they saw her coming. But Mr. Earl's tractor was huge. There was no way he could move to the shoulder of the road to get out of her way.

"Mama 'Cile. Mama 'Cile," I shouted. "That's Mr. Earl coming toward us. He's got that big plow. He can't scoot over. You have to move over, Mama 'Cile."

"He'll move," she said.

"But Mama 'Cile, that tractor is really big. He can't move over far enough. Please, Mama 'Cile. Move over."

Without saying a word or even glancing my way, she kept her eyes and the car right in the middle of the road, straddling that center line. As Mr. Earl and Mama 'Cile neared each other, I braced myself and felt my unborn child leap in my womb. At the last possible second, Mr. Earl jerked the tractor and plow to his right and went off the road, down a slight embankment, up the other side, down again, and back on the road behind us. I could read his lips as he jerked the tractor and plow out of the way. And what I read was not nice.

"I told you he'd move," Mama 'Cile said.

She stayed in the middle of Morella Road all the way to Anne's house. When we got there, I swung open the car door and fell to the ground. From the window of the house, Alan saw me go down and rushed outside. As he was helping me up, I began to cry and told him I would never ride with Mama 'Cile again.

She got out of her side of the car, came around to the front, looked down at me and said, "Well, I don't know what all the fuss is about. I told you he would move, and he did."

With an indignant toss of her head she marched into the house.

I never rode with Mama 'Cile again!

Mama's Wedding Day

By Joyce Milligan Tatum

One day after school I was sitting at the dining room table doing homework and watching the rain fall outside the window. My mother was working in the kitchen.

"Hey Mom!" I called out. "What was the weather like on your wedding day?

She came into the dining room and sat down in a chair across from me. "The weather on our wedding day?" she reminisced. "It was pretty. The sun was shining; and, for April, it was a warm day."

She stood up to go back to the kitchen, then turned to look at me. "Good thing it was nice weather," she said. "I sure would have hated to stand in the back of that wagon in the rain."

"What?" I was confused. "You were married at New Salem Church, right?"

"We were supposed to be married there," she replied, "but it didn't work out that way."

Then she proceeded to tell me the story. Daddy had gotten their marriage license in Trenton which is located in Gibson County. Back in the 1920s in Tennessee, a couple was required to marry in the county where they had gotten their marriage license. New Salem Church, the site for the wedding, is located in Obion County. The line between the two counties is roughly one-half mile from the church. The minister told my Daddy that, since the license was obtained in Gibson County, he couldn't marry them at the church located in Obion County. You can imagine how everyone reacted to that piece of news.

Fortunately, the great problem solver in the family, my mother's mother, came to the rescue. She told them all, including the minister, to get in the back of her wagon and go with her. She led everyone across the county line. The minister got in the wagon and went on with the ceremony. After this rustic ceremony, the wedding party and the guests went back to the church for the reception. And everyone lived happily ever after.

Pocahontas and the Train

By Joyce Milligan Tatum

Mason Hall is a very small community located in upper West Tennessee. It is halfway between Trimble, Tennessee which is on Highway 51 and Kenton, Tennessee, which is on Highway 45. Not too many people ever venture off one of those two highways to explore the area. Many years ago, when I was growing up, Mason Hall was a vibrant, active little farming town surrounded by corn and cotton fields. Almost everyone had a few acres where they grew their own vegetable gardens and fruit trees. Also, many people raised chickens and/or cows. It was the type of town in which a kid could get bored very easily.

One summer in my early teenage years, I was bored. Very bored! I was so bored I actually went with my father one Saturday morning to the Lodge where he served as a leader. He went inside, and I followed. One door in the building led into the actual meeting area; and, unless you were a member, you were not allowed in. I knew the rules and told my father that I would go upstairs and look around. He sternly told me, not to "get into anything."

The rooms upstairs had once served as Doctor Adams's office. He had passed away many years before, but all of his equipment was still there. When his office was open, people would enter the back of the building where a staircase led up to an outside door that took them directly into his office. We kids loved going to the office because he would let us play with Pocahontas, a skeleton made of heavy plastic that was wired together. Oddly enough, when I got upstairs, the door to the office was unlocked, so I waltzed right in. There was Pocahontas who had been neglected all these years. As I looked her over I came up with an idea.

When I got home, I rode my bike over to Michael's house where he and another friend, Terry, were playing ball.

"Hey guys," I called out. "I've got an idea for something we can do that will really scare some people."

Always up for mischief, they listened as I laid out my plan.

"You're crazy! "Michael said. "I like it, though."

Terry agreed, and together we "fine-tuned" the whole thing. That night, I got one of Daddy's flashlights and an old sheet from the linen closet. I slipped out of the house through my bedroom window. I had done it often enough so that I never got caught. I had put my bike next to the garage and quickly rode it to Michael's house. Terry was already there. Together we went over to the Lodge. Slipping in was easy. The basement windows were never locked, and once inside we went upstairs to Doc's office. There we wrapped Pocahontas in the sheet that I had brought with me.

She rattled as we took her downstairs and got her out of the building. Situating her on a bicycle took a little maneuvering, but we managed to take her to Terry's house where we hid her under some hay in the barn. Since the doctor's practice was closed, we knew no one would ever notice that she was missing.

The next morning after breakfast I went over to Michael's house. Terry came over shortly after. Together we finalized our plans for Pocahontas.

"My dad says the passenger train only comes by three times a week headed south and three times headed north," Terry said. "The southbound train comes by at 5:30 am, just about when the sun comes up; and the northbound train comes by at 5:00 pm. The southbound train comes through tomorrow morning."

"Looks like we are getting up early tomorrow morning, then," I said.

We agreed that if we got Pocahontas to the tracks around 4:00 am, we would be there in plenty of time to put her just in the right spot before the train came down the track and no one would see us. We could go back and get her later. We knew what we had to do.

Our plan was simple. The train track ran not far from Mason Hall through a swampy area of the Obion River. Unless you knew where to walk out there, you could be knee deep in mud in no time. Because it was summer time, the sun rose early, the perfect time for the train passengers to see Pocahontas if we placed her in the right place. We had an area picked out that was at least a mile from any homes, yet was close enough to the road so that we wouldn't have to walk very far. We agreed to meet at 2:30 am to start our plan.

I couldn't sleep that night. I kept watching the clock. At 2:00 am I slipped out of bed, put on my clothes, and out the window I went. I walked to Michael's house, skirting behind trees and houses along the way. Terry lived just two doors down from Michael's house. When I got to Michael's house, he and I ran over to Terry's, expecting him to be outside waiting for us. When we got there, he was nowhere to be seen. We couldn't find him anywhere.

"Just our luck!" I whispered. "He's probably still asleep."

"No, he's not," Michael whispered back, pointing to the barn. "There he is!"

Terry had already gotten Pocahontas out from under the hay. He had wrapped her in a sheet like a mummy and put her in a wheelbarrow; and, fortunately, he had a flashlight.

"Let's go," he said.

We followed Terry as he wheeled Pocahontas toward our agreed upon destination. We tried to be as quiet as possible, hoping that no one in the houses nearby could hear the rattling sound coming from Pocahontas.

It's a good mile or more from Terry's house to the spot we had picked out. Terry led us through the swampy area where the flashlight helped us keep away from the most treacherous places. When we got to our chosen location, we took Pocahontas out of the wheelbarrow; and the three of us carried her to the tracks. We left the wheelbarrow in a ditch at the edge of the swamp because we would need it later when we retrieved Pocahontas from the place where we left her. About fifteen feet from the tracks stood a large tree with some very low limbs. We unwrapped Pocahontas from the sheet. With twine Terry had taken from the barn, we tied her to the tree as though she were standing up. We situated her carefully so that not only the light of the rising sun but the light of the train coming around a curve would shine on her for all to see.

"Perfect," we three agreed.

We left Pocahontas standing there. Each of us went back to our respective homes and waited. I heard the train whistle and looked at my clock – right on time – 5:30 am.

The southbound train left Chicago in the late afternoon and traveled all night on the way to its final destination of New Orleans. It made five stops along the way. Pocahontas was located between the second and third stop. From her position alongside the track, it would take another forty-five minutes to an hour before the train would stop again.

When I heard the train whistle, I jumped out of bed; and since I had gone to bed in my clothes, I was ready to scoot out the window and retrieve Pocahontas. As I ran toward Michael's house, I saw both him and Terry ready to go. We ran toward the tracks, got Pocahontas untied, wrapped her back up in the sheet, and gathered up the twine. We carried her from the swamp to the wheelbarrow and hurried back to the barn. With Pocahontas safely hidden away, we went home.

My older brother Daniel who was a sheriff's deputy came over to the house later that morning. I heard him telling my mother that he had to go down to the tracks early that morning because some people on the train thought they saw a skeleton standing next to a tree.

"Crazy people!" he said. "It was just getting daylight and they think they see a skeleton out there in that swamp. There wasn't anything out there. We spent two hours looking for nothing."

I smiled knowing there would be something there the next day.

We continued our game off and on for several weeks. Not every night, but at random times. After a couple of weeks, we decided to stay out there one night to watch the train. On that particular night, I had brought one of my mother's bonnets with me and an old bucket with a handle. We tied the bonnet on Pocahontas, put the bucket on her arm, and sat her on the ground with her legs crossed. When the train whistle blew, we were hiding behind some big cypress trees watching. The lights were all on inside the train. The people were pressed against the window looking out. It was misty that morning with the fog rolling in, giving an eerie appearance to everything. The train slowed down. The light from the train beamed right on Pocahontas. People were pointing.

My father had been reading in the newspaper about the strange sightings and how investigators had no clue about how a skeleton wound up in that swamp. He remarked to my mother that it must be a bunch of kids pulling a practical joke of some kind. I never said a word to anyone except Michael and Terry. We had a great time fooling the sheriff's department and the people on the train, but soon we got tired of getting up and sneaking out of the house so early in the morning. We were afraid that sooner or later we were going to get caught if we didn't quit while we were ahead.

School would soon begin, and we knew we had to get rid of Pocahontas. She had begun to show some pretty drastic signs of aging from all the rough treatment she had been through. We were afraid we would get caught if we tried to take her back to Doctor Adams's old office, so we decided to put her under the bridge at Grassy Creek. We knew she would ultimately be found there and perhaps would be given a good home somewhere. We barely managed to get her under the bridge so that anyone who looked down while traveling over the bridge would see her arm and head sticking out and stop to investigate. We said our goodbyes to her and went home.

School started. Every day we traveled over that bridge on the school bus. The first few days we looked over the edge to try to spy Pocahontas, but we never had any luck. Soon we lost interest as the school year progressed. Fall turned into winter and winter into spring.

That spring we had some serious rainfall for almost two weeks solid. At one point, there was so much flooding that school was canceled for two days. Early on the second day of the school cancellation, my father got a phone call from the sheriff's department. It was my brother Daniel, who worked there, calling my Dad to let him know about a skeleton that had washed up from Grassy Creek into the front yard of a home that a couple rented from my father. Since my father owned that home, he told Daniel that he would be right over. I went with him.

When we arrived at the couple's house, there were two deputy cars, the sheriff's car, and numerous other people who had arrived to see the skeleton. As I soon as I saw it, I knew it was her. There lay Pocahontas minus her head.

Without thinking I gasped, "Pocahontas!"

My father gave me a funny look.

"I mean, well, it looks like that skeleton that was in Doctor Adams' office. I saw it there once. 'Course when I saw her, she had a head," I stammered.

My brother Daniel walked up to my dad. I tried to remain calm, knowing that I may have accidentally gotten myself in a lot of trouble.

"That thing just washed up here from the creek over there," Daniel pointed out. He pointed to the swollen creek. "We don't know where it came from or where it belongs. It's a fake one, and it is missing a lot of parts."

My father looked from Daniel to me. "I think I might have a clue. It does look kind of like the one from Doctor Adams's old office. Somebody might have stolen it and put it somewhere so it would scare people."

We went home soon afterward; and except for an article in the newspaper about the incident, not another word was ever spoken in our house about Pocahontas. I have no idea where her head ended up. Grassy Creek empties into the Obion River and eventually into the Forked Deer River and from there into the Mississippi River. I figure it will turn up down river somewhere someday and maybe scare somebody half to death.

Hurricane Katrina in Tennessee

By Joyce Milligan Tatum

As we watched the news about Hurricane Katrina in late August of 2005, my husband, Alan, and I wondered how we could help. We discussed sending money to the Red Cross or gathering food items or clothing to send. Little did we know that less than 24 hours later God would show us what to do.

A group of mentally and physically challenged individuals from a residential home, along with their caregivers and other family members, had left their home in New Orleans on a bus heading north to escape the storm. When they left, it was thought that the storm was moving in another direction and that New Orleans would not take a direct hit. Even so, the staff of the home decided to take no chances and evacuate. Each staff person supervising these challenged individuals was allowed to bring two family members, enough clothes for three days, along with food and a bottle of water. They were hoping to return home within 72 hours, so most of them had only a three-day supply of their medications. We know now that their supply would prove to be inadequate.

The youngest of the group was eight months old, and the oldest was seventy-one. They had driven northeast for several hundred miles when they reached Chattanooga, Tennessee, where they had arranged to stop at a local hospital. There some people were seen by a physician. By this time, they had been on the road for 24 hours with no hope of returning to New Orleans any time soon. The hospital staff had seen the story of the disaster on television and told the travelers it was not possible for them to go home at that time. Because none of them had serious illnesses or injuries, they were unable to stay at the hospital for a long period of time. However, local hospital people made phone calls and arranged for the group go to Fall Creek Falls, a state park about 70 miles north from Chattanooga. Once again, they headed north and ended up at Fall Creek Falls State Park, in the high hills just south of Spencer, Tennessee. There they would spend at least one night, and maybe more.

By this time, people were running out of their regular medications, but it was arranged for the hospital to send some of the medicine to Fall Creek Falls. The park provided a group camp with a large dormitory and separate eating facilities for the displaced individuals. They had very little food, no clean clothing, and almost no medicine in the middle of strange surroundings. The park had no television, so they could not find out what was happening in their home city. Even worse, there was only one pay phone in the whole building. Over half of the 22,000 acres Fall Creek Falls is a natural wilderness area. It is very remote. Cell phones did not work in the park. Because the group arrived at night, the majority of them had no idea where they were. It was as if they had landed in another world.

After the group arrived, the park manager, who had been called by the hospital personnel, arrived and quickly realized these people needed major help. Even though it was the middle of the night, he made several phone calls to other employees, and things began to happen. Park employees came from their homes and brought food for the group that night and gathered needed supplies.

The next morning, as word got out in the communities surrounding the state park, local church members began to arrive with food and clothing. A public health nurse and her staff brought medical supplies. My husband, Alan, who is a pharmacist, was called because some much-needed medicine for the people had not arrived from Chattanooga. When called, no one hesitated. Everyone went to work to help in any way they could. The park received over 150 phone calls from people in the area who were willing to help.

Alan and I arrived at Fall Creek Falls on Wednesday afternoon with much needed medicine. Children were crying, patients were upset, and the staff was "plumb wore out" (as we say in Tennessee). The Wal-Mart, some 30 miles away, had loaned the travelers a large screen television to be set up in the recreation room. A local cable company sent out a television with equipment and a technician to set it up so that the staff could see what was happening in New Orleans. Alan and I were there when the television first came on. Everyone gathered around the set. That is something I will never forget. Those people were seeing for the first time the devastating aftermath of Katrina. A stunned silence filled the room. I could not imagine how those people must have felt. Then came the sobs and the heartbreak that they felt after seeing their homes and perhaps even their families gone. I held people as they cried, as they tried to figure out what to do next. They were stranded here in the mountains of Tennessee, not knowing where their families were or even if they were alive. The staff continued to take care of these disabled people whose needs were so great. They tried not to let their own emotions show.

When the evacuation of New Orleans began, many of the staff brought their children with them. These children had nothing to do. They were from the city, after all, and the woods of Tennessee looked like a dangerous place to be. Alan and I made a trip to Wal-Mart and purchased individual CD players and CD's. We bought another television set along with a PlayStation and hand held games for children and teenagers. We called our friends at our church. Phone cards began to arrive so that the staff had a way to call from the pay phone. People brought board games, balls, stuffed animals, toys, baby clothes, and diapers (one staff member had her eight-month old grandson with her). The people of the Upper Cumberland Region in Tennessee were remarkable. Everywhere Alan and I went, people wanted to help.

It was Labor Day weekend. Two of the children became ill and needed medical attention. Alan called a car dealership in Sparta, just a few miles north of Fall Creek Falls, to see about renting a large van to transport the children and their families to the doctor. The owner of the dealership told us to come to the lot and just take one. He even made sure the van was full of gas. Two pediatricians agreed to see the children at no charge. We went to Fall Creek Falls and brought parents and children down the mountain to the doctor's office in Sparta. After the doctor's visit, we brought the two families to our home for an afternoon of rest. They were able to get on the computer and try to find other family members. They were able to use the phone without someone standing over them waiting for his or her turn. They were able to relax, and the children were able to play and run. They spent the night with us.

One of the senior staff members with the group from New Orleans located a place in Nashville that offered its facilities for the group to use for two weeks.

On Tuesday, everyone began the move to the center in Nashville. We arrived at Fall Creek Falls early in the morning and packed our van with things that had been given to individual people. Someone had made a huge banner and had it taped to the side of the bus filled with the people from New Orleans. The sign said "Thank you Tennessee! We are from New Orleans!" A Tennessee Highway Patrol officer led the caravan, followed by the bus and five additional vehicles, all filled with donations. We began our trip toward Nashville. At a truck stop, people asked about our group. Some of them gave us money to give to the staff. Another person offered to buy everyone lunch. Truck drivers offered to fill the bus with gas using their own personal credit cards.

The staff from New Orleans had made hand held signs that said, "We are from New Orleans. Thank you, Tennessee" and "We love you Tennessee! Thank you!" Almost everyone had small American flags and a few even had Tennessee flags provided by the Fall Creek Falls staff. The patients and staff waved these flags out the bus windows. Our group looked like a parade going down the interstate. Other motorists were waving and blowing their car and truck horns. I had never seen anything like it.

The development center in Nashville welcomed them with open arms. They furnished large rooms for each staff family along with bunk beds for the children. There was a playground where the children could run and play. The patients had living areas with room where they could move around. They could go outside to a secure area without staff worrying about the patients getting lost. The center also provided respite care for the staff so that they could take some time off – something they needed desperately.

Alan and I became close to the two families that stayed with us. They were finally able to return to their beloved New Orleans. They lost their homes and some family members to the storm, but they have rebuilt their lives. Alan and I will never forget them.

Friends in High Places

By Suellen Alfred

It was Friday night. Leonard could not get his daddy's car. In fact, none of the guys could get his daddy's car, so the boys were left to walk wherever they went. As they were ambling toward the center of town, Chris had a brain storm.

"Hey, I got an idea." Chris was always full of ideas, and some of them even made sense. "This week in auto mechanics at school we have been working on this guy's car. He left it in the parking lot over the weekend so it would be there early on Monday morning, ready for us to work on. I know where the keys are. Let's go get it."

It did not take them long to get to the garage of the high school auto mechanics department. Sure enough, Chris found the keys. And for a while they argued about who was going to drive. The boys finally agreed that Chris should drive because he was the one who found the car for them. Everyone piled in the car. Away they went, riding around town, shouting at girls, and feeling good. It never dawned on them that they were breaking the law by actually "borrowing" this car.

After a while, some genius suggested they drive down an unpaved road on the outskirts of town. That road had no street lights. There was no moon that night, and the road was very steep and curvy. Now, nobody knows whether they were drinking, but Bill swears they were not. Chris was just driving too fast and missed a turn. The next thing they knew, they were in the ditch. Try as they might, the boys could not move the car back on the road. There was nothing to do but walk back home. Every man for himself. There is no honor among thieves. Those boys scattered in all direction. At this point, we don't know what happened to any of the boys except Bill, and all we know is what Bill told us.

Bill did not know where those guys went. He wasn't concerned with them. He was concerned about the damage his face sustained after he took a bite out of the dashboard when the car crashed. His face was a bloody mess. He walked back to the main road and started hitch hiking to the hospital. He walked for what seemed to be a very long time until finally some sympathetic citizen picked him up and took him to the emergency room.

When he got to the hospital, he was bleeding badly enough that the nurse signed him in at once. Now that he was safely at the hospital, he started worrying about what his parents were going to say. Maybe, he thought, they will be in bed when I get home. In the morning, when they ask about what happened, I'll tell them that I got into a fight. That will sound better than wrecking somebody's car. Immediately after that thought went through his head, he had something really to worry about when he saw two policemen enter the emergency room. Bill had a pretty good idea about why they were there. To this day, he has no idea how they knew he was at the hospital. As luck would have it, Dr. England was working at the emergency room that night. He lived next door to Bill's family and knew Bill well. The timing could not have been more perfect. Dr. England came into the waiting room just as the police were trying to usher Bill out the door to the police car waiting outside.

"What's going on here?" the doctor asked.

"We have come to arrest this boy. We have reason to believe that he was involved in the theft of an automobile earlier tonight. This kid is going to jail."

"He is not going anywhere," Dr. England said, in a very authoritative voice. "This boy is my patient. He needs immediate medical attention. I may even have to admit him to the hospital. I suggest you men go back to the station."

Bill was astonished to see the police officers meekly turn around and leave the room. As far as he remembers, he was never arrested, and he does not know why. When someone asked what his parents said when he got home from the hospital, he said their reaction must have been pretty bad because he has repressed that memory. But he certainly remembers that it pays to know friends in high places.

I'm Sorry, We're Closed

By Suellen Alfred

Believe it or not, in the early 1980s, I was alive and kicking in a time when few people had what came to be known as a personal computer. Now, everyone has a computer, and a load of information is at our fingertips. But in the early eighties, if I needed to send something from one city to another I sent it through the mail – snail mail as it is sometimes known. Faxing a document or sending it as an attachment to an e-mail message was unheard of in my town. If I needed information, I actually had to go to the library or call people on the telephone in order to find out what I needed to know. If I wanted to find a local person's phone number – that is, the kind of phone that plugged into the wall, the kind we now call a land line – I used the phone book which was published by the phone company and given free to everyone who had a phone. If the number was not in the phone book, I called directory assistance. If I needed a zip code for a person's address, I called the post office. And that is where this story begins and ends.

Late one afternoon I had just written a letter - on real paper with a real pen (what some folks in the South call an "ink pen"), in cursive handwriting, which I understand to my great horror is no longer being taught in some schools. When it came time to address the envelope, I had the recipient's address, but I did not know the zip code. Now, remember, this was in the day and the place before people used computers to tell them everything they needed to know. So, in order to obtain the zip code, I used the most advanced technology I had, the phone, what we now call the land line. I called the post office. I knew that the post office closed at 5:00 pm, and I knew I had to make the call pretty quickly as the clock showed the time to be around 4:55. I just hoped I could reach somebody by phone before the five o'clock closing time. I thought I was in luck when a pleasant person answered, "Good afternoon, Talbott Post Office."

Great, I thought. Now I can find out the zip code for this letter and get it off in tomorrow's mail.

"Good afternoon," I said. "Can you give me the. . ."

"I'm sorry, we're closed," she said.

"No, you don't understand. I just need the zip. . ."

"I'm sorry, we're closed."

"This won't take long. Can you. . ."

"I'm sorry. We're closed." Spoken in a monotone like an ancient mantra, the disembodied voice on the other end of the phone sounded like a robot.

"Well, if you are closed, why did you answer the phone?" By this time, I had failed to keep the sense of frustration out of my voice.

"Because I thought somebody might want to talk to me."

Now my irritation quickly exploded into the sound of angry disbelief. I could hear myself shouting, "Well, **I** want to talk to you. Can you. . "

"I'm sorry, we're closed." I couldn't believe it. I rudely hung up the phone without even saying thank you.

The next day I actually drove to the post office where I obtained the requisite zip code and mailed my letter!

I suspect that when the woman said, "I thought somebody might want to talk to me," she was expecting to hear the voice of a child or a spouse, or some other family member on the other end of the line. A pesky customer looking for a zip code was the last thing on her mind, and she was not about to work one minute over time.

The Legend of Reelfoot Lake

By Joyce Milligan Tatum

Reelfoot Lake is a shallow lake located in upper West Tennessee. The lake was formed by a series of earthquakes that occurred from December of 1811 until March of 1812. Three massive earthquakes and hundreds of tremors changed the course of the Mississippi River and caused swamps and lakes to form over the land. Over eighteen thousand acres of swamps and lakes joined together to form Reelfoot Lake. As you can imagine, a great number of stories about the lake have developed over the last two hundred years. This story came from my father.

It was Indian country. In the days before Reelfoot Lake was formed, a Chickasaw tribe, according to legend, lived in the area where the lake now exists. A young warrior, the son of a chief, had been born with a deformed foot causing him to walk with a rolling gait. The people called him Reelfoot. When his father died, Reelfoot became chief.

In the spring of 1811, Reelfoot and some of the other warriors from his tribe traveled south into Choctaw country. They met the Choctaw Chief who had a beautiful daughter. Reelfoot fell in love with the young maiden, but her father would not hear of his daughter having anything to do with this deformed young man. He ordered Reelfoot to go back to his home and think no more of his daughter. Reelfoot offered many treasures to the chief in exchange for the fair maiden, but the chief was not impressed and called upon the Great Spirit to reason with Reelfoot. The Great Spirit told Reelfoot that no Indian should take a wife from another tribe, because if he married the Choctaw chief's daughter, the Great Spirit would destroy Reelfoot's village.

Reelfoot went home greatly frightened by what the Great Spirit had told him. But as time went on, he began to question the Great Spirit and soon convinced himself that if he married the Choctaw maiden, the Great Spirit would not harm him or his people. His logic, if there is such a thing in matters of love, told him that the Great Spirit had already made him deformed, and thus would not hurt him anymore.

In the early fall, Reelfoot gathered several warriors together and went back to the Choctaw village. In spite of the disapproval of both her father and the Great Spirit, Reelfoot took the young maiden back home with him (Apparently, it did not occur to him to ask the maiden what she wanted to do.) She had heard what the Great Spirit had said, and she was very frightened. She asked Reelfoot to take her back to her people. Reelfoot refused. He and the young maiden arrived back at the Chickasaw village where he announced that he had brought home a wife. He asked that the village launch a festival to celebrate his marriage. As the village prepared for the celebration, the warriors who traveled with Reelfoot to the Choctaw camp the first time remembered what the Great Spirit had said. Fearing that great trouble would come to pass, many of them disappeared from the village, taking refuge far from their home.

As the celebration was taking place, the Great Spirit became angry. The Great Spirit caused the earth to shake and reel. The Spirit stomped his foot in anger three separate times, causing the waters of the Mississippi River to back up and cover Reelfoot's land. Reelfoot, the Choctaw maiden, and, except the warriors who were wise enough to leave the area, all the people of the village were drowned. Now they all lie beneath the waters of Reelfoot Lake.

In the late fall, it is said that if you stand next to the water's edge late at night and listen very closely, you will hear the cries of the Choctaw people. It is also said that when the moon shines bright on the waters of the Lake you can see Reelfoot walking with his rolling gait looking for the Choctaw maiden.

Out of the Mouths of Babes

By Joyce Milligan Tatum

(The names of the children in this story have been changed, but they and their parents will know who they are.)

For over twenty-five years I worked with children. I served as a children's storyteller at the local library, and as a preschool teacher and administrator at a local church nursery school. I have worked in the public school system as well. Working with children can give you a unique perspective on life. Their reasoning process – or lack thereof – never ceased to amaze me, and their attempts to describe what they are thinking or doing during the day were often hysterical.

At school, we had children with parents from every occupation. From college professors to farmers and from doctors to factory workers. We loved them all - children and parents.

***

One morning a police officer brought his daughter to school and as he was leaving he stopped by my office.

"Good morning," I greeted him. He looked around just outside my office door to see if anyone was around.

"Miss Joyce, I need some help, please. You know Jane (his wife's name) is out of town and I'm keeping the girls until she gets back, he said.

"Yes, I know. Is there a problem?"

He hurriedly reassured me "No! No! The girls are fine. I love keeping them, and we are having a great time. I just need to know how to remove nail polish."

"From clothes," I asked?

"No. From toe nails," he replied.

"Jane won't mind that you painted their toe nails. She has done it several times, and she uses the brightest colors. The girls love it."

He sheepishly answered, "It's not *their* toe nails. It's mine. I got ready for bed last night and sat down in the recliner. The girls were still up watching TV, and I guess I dozed off. I must have slept hard because the girls painted my toe nails 'Harlot Red'. I didn't notice it until I got up this morning. They think it's funny, but if the guys at the station find out they'll really give me a hard time. I need to get this stuff off."

Before me stood one of the toughest, strongest police officers I have ever known; and he was worried about his painted toe nails! I tried to keep the grin off my face.

Biting my lower lip, I explained nail polish remover, how to use it and where to buy it.

The next morning when he brought his youngest daughter to school he gave me a big smile and a thumb up.

In my job, you had to be prepared for anything.

***

Patrick was a precious five-year-old who was quite active and was never at a loss for words. His very devoted grandparents loved to spend time with him. He was planning to spend the weekend with them, and he arrived at school on Friday with bag packed and a life jacket.

"Patrick," I asked, "Why are you taking your life jacket with you?"

With his usual exuberance he replied, "I'm going to the aquarium, and my mom doesn't want me to take any chances."

***

Quinton had been absent for a week with the chicken pox. The following week, I was on vacation, and the week after that Quinton was on vacation. So, it had been three weeks since I had seen him. When he arrived at school he appeared to have grown quite a bit taller.

My goodness, Quinton," I said. "You have grown another foot. "He quickly looked down at his feet and said very casually, "I did not. I still have only these two."

***

Early on a Thursday morning, just before Easter, one of the teachers asked a friend to bring Mr. Biggs, a very large white rabbit, to school and put it in the courtyard which was an enclosed area surrounded by two classrooms with lots of windows, a fellowship hall, and a hallway, both of which had walls that were all glass. We didn't tell the children the rabbit was there, but it didn't take long for them to see Itoh, the excitement it caused!

"It's the Easter Bunny!"

"How did he get out there?"

"Did he bring any candy?"

"Where's his mama?"

"Can we feed him?"

The list of questions was endless.

The pre-kindergarten kids were all four and five-year-olds who can go the restroom without supervision. One young man, John David, exercised that right. John David did not go to the restroom. Instead, he went to the door of the courtyard. Of course, when he opened that door, Mr. Biggs hopped right in. He kept on hopping down the hallway, past the Minister of Music's office and into the sanctuary.

John David came running into my office to tell me that the rabbit had "run off to church. "Once I realized what John David had done, I took off for the sanctuary, grabbing two teaching assistants on the way to help. The search was on, and I can tell you that searching for a white rabbit in a very large sanctuary was an arduous task. We finally located Mr. Biggs under some pews and got him back to the courtyard. I called the custodian and explained to him what the pellets in the sanctuary were. I dared not ask him what he was thinking as together he and I cleaned the carpet. I am sure that was the first and only time the custodian ever cleaned up rabbit poop from the floor in a house of worship. Oh well, "all creatures great and small. . ."

***

A local farmer brought a baby lamb to school and left the animal with us for the children to see. The lamb was taken out into the courtyard which is about twenty feet by forty feet with two trees and shrubs in itched jumped and played in the courtyard much to the children's delight. After three hours, the farmer returned to pick up the lamb. When he opened the door to the courtyard, like the rabbit before him, the lamb darted inside the building. The farmer, three teachers, twenty-something children, and I gave chase. A lamb can run fast when chased by screaming children. We finally caught him in the kitchen. The farmer picked him up and started for the exit door. The children were all shouting "Bye."

The lamb leaned over the farmer's shoulder and said, "Bae."

To this day, the children swear he said "Bye" to them; and I suspect they are right.

***

One day as a surprise for the children and the teachers, I arranged for a baby elephant from a traveling circus to visit. When the trainer and Elsie arrived, the trainer unloaded her from the trailer. Without informing me that he was there, trainer and elephant proceeded to come into the church and down the hall to the nursery school end of the building.

I was in my office when I began hearing screams and laughter. When I stepped out into the hallway, I saw coming toward me the trainer, the baby elephant, and the children, in that order. I turned the whole parade around and got them all back outside where Elsie spent the next hour with the children. The minister never knew that an elephant had been in his church. All in a day's work.

* * *

Stephen came in after recess covered with dirt. "Stephen, why do you always get so dirty on the playground?" I asked.

"I don't know. I guess the dirt just likes me," he answered.

* * *

One day at circle time, I asked the children what they did every day before they ate dinner. We were studying germs, and I was hoping they would tell me that they always wash their hands.

Rachel piped up and said, "We always pray."

"Why do you pray?" one child asked.

Rachel replied, "Daddy says we have to 'because Mommy isn't a very good cook."

* * *

Andrew was muttering something one morning, but I couldn't understand what he was saying.

"Andrew, what are you saying, sweetie?" I asked.

"Up and at 'em! Up and at 'em!" he replied. "Why does my mom say that every morning? Doesn't she know that my name is Andrew, not Adam?"

* * *

Oliver was my red-headed firecracker who loved to jump off anything. One morning he arrived at school with a broken right arm. It seems that the night before, he had jumped off the top bunk of his bed and hit the chest of drawers on the way down. He was in a cast for six weeks. His mother picked him up from school early on a Wednesday afternoon to take him to the doctor to have the cast removed. The next morning, he arrived at school with a cast on his left arm. His mother told me that within an hour after he got home from the doctor's office the day before, he jumped off the back of the couch and hit the coffee table on the way down.

* * *

Matt was doing his usual running without looking where he was going. He ran right into the edge of the door. It left quite a knot on his head. He was crying when the teacher brought him into my office. I picked him up and rocked him while the teacher made a call to his mother.

As I was rocking Matt, I said, "Oh Matt! Running into that door must have made you really mad."

"No, it didn't," he said. "It made me cry."

* * *

One day we had "Sloppy Joes" on sesame seed buns for lunch. Ben was at my table picking the seeds off the top of the bun.

"Ben, don't you like sesame seed buns?" I asked.

"Oh yes, Miss Joyce, I really like them. I'm going to take these homes to plant them in my yard and grow a sesame tree.

* * *

It had been raining all week, and the children were getting restless from too much indoor time. The teachers needed a break, so I volunteered to take the children for a walk around the church. We had quite a parade, marching up the hallway, out on the covered balcony in the back, down to the basement to explore, and then back upstairs by the sanctuary. The foyer wall just outside the sanctuary was solid from the floor up to about three feet. On top of that short wall was a solid glass wall that extends to the ceiling, giving people a nice view of the sanctuary. As we were quietly walking back toward the nursery school end of the building, two of the little boys stopped and pressed their faces to the glass to look in.

"Wow! What is this place?" Cody asked.

"That's God's house," Jimmy said.

"I don't see God in there," Cody said.

"Of course, you don't," said Jimmy. "He's a Holy Ghost."

I had to walk away.

Salad Girl

By Jennie Ivey

(This story appeared originally in two parts on December 6 and December 13, 2015, in the *Herald Citizen*, for which Jennie Ivey writes a weekly column in Cookeville, Tennessee.)

As every fall semester winds, down and students scramble for Christmas-break jobs, I remember a three-week holiday stint at the Western Sizzling' Steak House when I was a junior in college.

It was 1974, and salad bars had not yet come into vogue. Not in Nashville, Tennessee, anyway. I was to be the Sizzling' "salad girl," making the grand sum of $2. 10 an hour. No tips. After customers took a tray, silverware and a paper napkin from the START HERE station, they began traveling down the serving line and peering through the Plexiglas barrier that separated them from the kitchen staff and the food. They came to me first.

"Would you care for a salad tonight?" I'd ask in my friendliest voice.

If the customer said yes, and they almost always did, I would hand them a flimsy faux-wood bowl pre-filled with iceberg lettuce, shredded carrots, two wedges of winter tomato and croutons that came straight from a box. I know they came straight from a box because I was the one who had prepared the salads half an hour earlier.

"What kind of dressing would you like?"

But before I could rattle off the list, the customer usually interrupted to say, "What are my choices?"

"French, Italian, Thousand Island, and Bleu Cheese."

"Catalina French or regular French?"

"Regular."

"No Green Goddess?"

"Sorry. No."

"Then give me Thousand Island. Double scoop."

Funny thing was, back then almost everybody wanted Thousand Island dressing on their salad. Nowadays, I don't even know if you can find such a thing in a restaurant unless you're ordering a Reuben sandwich. I suppose its popularity waned when Ranch dressing came onto the scene, though I don't know that for sure.

After departing my station, customers moved down the line to order their steak, which was immediately slapped onto the hot griddle. Then they were handed a foil-wrapped baked potato (with butter AND sour cream at no extra charge) and chose a dessert and drink. By the time, they reached the end of the line and paid the cashier, the steak was ready.

The system was extraordinarily efficient. I don't know how many customers we served during the typical dinner hour, but it was aplenty. My first night on the job, a Friday I believe, I served salads for four solid hours without a break. It was mind-numbingly boring. But I kept a smile on my face and a lilt in my voice and couldn't understand why, as closing time approached, the restaurant manager motioned me into to his tiny office in the back corner of the kitchen.

"Close the door, please," he said, settling down into his desk chair. "I'd like to talk to you."

My heart was hammering. Was I in trouble? Had I done something wrong? Was I about to be fired from my lucrative Christmas-break job?

So here I was, standing in the manager's tiny office at Western Sizzling' Steak House a couple of weeks before Christmas 1974, wondering if I was about to be fired after my first evening on the job. I sank into the dented folding chair across from Mr. Williams's desk. "Am I in trouble?" I stammered.

"No, no, not at all," he assured me. "I just want to compliment you on the wonderful job you've done tonight. You're one of the fastest learners we've ever had on the kitchen staff."

Dumbfounded, I stared at him. "There wasn't much to learn," I finally said.

"Not true," he said. "I watched you count out exactly six croutons for each salad, just like you were taught. And you rattled off the salad dressing choices without missing a beat."

Was he kidding me? If two-and-a-half years of college hadn't prepared me to count croutons and memorize a list of four dressings, my parents were wasting a whole lot of money on my tuition. I didn't say that, of course. I just thanked Mr. Williams and said I'd see him tomorrow. Crystal, the assistant manager who'd been the one to train me in salad girl skills, was standing just outside the office door as I emerged. "What were you doing in there?" she asked in an accusatory tone of voice.

"Nothing." I shrugged and headed for the lockers to get my coat.

From that moment on and for reasons I'll never understand, Crystal seemed to have it in for me. She began taping up signs in the kitchen. Signs that said things like MAKE SURE REFRIGERATOR DOOR IS CLOSED and PUT USED PAPER TOWELS IN TRASH CAN and MOP UP ALL SPILLS. She always signed them "The *mangement*," which I took to mean "The Management." Wisely, I chose not to point out the misspelling to her. Or to ask why we needed those stupid signs.

Crystal found fault with everything I did. I put too much salad dressing on one customer's lettuce, not enough on another. One night as I was helping a co-worker wrap potatoes in aluminum foil, she snatched the foil from my hands. "This," she said, "is how you wrap a potato." Then she proceeded to do it the same way I had.

The last straw came two days before the job was scheduled to end. Just before the restaurant was to close for the night, Crystal put me to work slicing lemons for iced tea. Then she stood over my shoulder, watching and criticizing. Finally, I'd had enough. "I'm twenty-one years old," I told her, "and I don't need MANGE-ment to tell me how to cut a lemon!" With that, the knife slipped and nicked the index finger of my left hand. Blood spurted everywhere. Crystal screamed. Mr. Williams came charging out of his office. When he saw, what had happened, he pulled a none-too-clean handkerchief out of his pocket and tried to wrap it around my finger.

"I'm done," I told him, replacing his handkerchief with a somewhat cleaner napkin. "I know I'm supposed to work for two more days, but I just can't take it anymore." I walked to the sink and ran water over my finger, which really wasn't cut all that badly. "I'm sorry, Mr. Williams, but I quit."

And to this day, I can't slice a lemon or hear someone ask for Thousand Island dressing without remembering that long-ago Christmas and my short-lived career as a Sizzling' salad girl.

Pee Can Pie

By Joyce Milligan Tatum

Several years back, my husband, Alan, and I were in Canada having dinner at a very elegant restaurant. I did my best to behave, but sometimes a Southern girl just must correct someone who clearly has pronunciation difficulties.

The dessert cart came to our table, and a very elegant waiter began to describe the wonderful items.

"Ah, madam. We have chocolate mousse, sorbet in a variety of flavors, apple pie, and lemon meringue pie."

And then he said, "We have Pecan pie," with an emphasis on the first syllable. He pronounced the second syllable as if he were referring to can of peaches.

"What did you call that?"

"Pecan pie. It is a type of nut, I believe, found in the southern part of the United States."

Alan knew what was about to happen. I could tell by the way he rolled his eyes and shook his head.

"Honey," I said. "I am from the South, and that is not **PEE** can."

He looked at me in bewilderment.

"A pee can be what is kept under your bed at night, so when you wake up and have to go, you don't have to put on your shoes and coat and go outside to the outhouse. That nut is pronounced 'pec**an**'."

The waiter looked very surprised. His mouth fell open, and he turned a few shades of red. However, he quickly regained his composure and immediately moved on to the next table without waiting for our order.

I heard him as he began to list the desserts for the people there. As he got to the list of pies, I watched and listened closely. When he said the word "**PEE** can" he looked up and saw me watching him.

Quickly he corrected himself and said "pec**an**." "I smiled and nodded.

Alan said, "You know we will not be getting any dessert. After what you just told him, he won't come back to our table. "He was right; the waiter didn't come back, and I was really wanting to try the sorbet, too.

What Did You Say? Miscommunication in East Tennessee

By Suellen Alfred

Sometimes personal stories are so short they are really only anecdotes that can be told in the span of just a few minutes. At least that is the case with so many of my friends whom I have known for a very long time. Several times a year, my friends and I get together, sometimes for a special occasion and sometimes just for the fun of it. Every time we do, we are sure to hear entertaining stories from just about everyone in the room.

Here are some of the anecdotes Dennie Ruth Kelley shared at a recent get together.

Dennie Ruth is from Alabama where she grew up with a very thick southern accent. One summer her mother and father drove her and her younger brother from Alabama to New Jersey to visit friends and family. Not long after they got there, her brother went missing. The whole family searched the neighborhood for him. After looking for quite a while, they finally came upon a group of boys asking kids to pay an entrance fee to go into their garage. Upon further investigation, the parents discovered that the boys were charging kids in the neighborhood a dime a piece to come into the garage and listen to this Alabama kid with the thick Southern accent say, "One tater, two taters, three taters, four." The lost brother was found.

* * *

Church services are rich fodder for funny stories. Dennie Ruth Kelly tells the story of a little boy who had never been to a funeral. At the first funeral service he had ever attended, he looked around in awe at the great number of people who had gathered in the sanctuary. He kept looking around intently as if he were searching for a specific person. After a few minutes of apparent frustration, he said to his mother, "Well, I see all these people here, but don't you think God should be here, too?"

* * *

Dennie Ruth told another story of a kid at a funeral service who really did not understand what was going on. All he knew was that the people were gathered in the church to listen to somebody talk. After the service was over, the kid could be heard grumbling. "That's the worst picnic I ever saw. They didn't even have any food."

* * *

At another church gathering, members of the church were given frozen turkeys for Thanksgiving. Some of the young people were asked to help people carry the turkeys to the altar where the minister said a prayer of thanksgiving over them. Every Sunday, at the beginning of the service, the pastor asks the children in the congregation to come to the front of the sanctuary to tell them a story. The story that day centered around Jesus's ministry of helping people who are hungry and giving to the poor. At the end of the children's lesson, the pastor asked, "What do you think Jesus would do with these turkeys?" He was anticipating the children would answer, "Give them to the poor." One kid, who had helped carry the heavy frozen birds to the altar said, "Well, I guess if Jesus were here, he would raise all these turkeys from the dead." The people in the congregation laughed until tears ran down their faces.

* * *

When Jean Robinson and her husband first moved to Knoxville from California, they quickly located a house to rent. When they moved in, they found that the house was replete with fleas. Jean called the landlady, and asked her to call an exterminator. The woman readily agreed. She then asked her, "Do you have any spahders?"

"I beg your pardon? Jean asked.

"Spahders. Does the house have any spahders?" she asked.

Jean had no idea what he was talking about. Spahders? What are they? Are they dangerous?"

"Some of them can be," she said.

"Well, what are spahders?" Jean asked.

"Well, you know," she said. "They make webs."

Jean did not understand the landlady's East Tennessee pronunciation of "spiders."

Hoopin Pine Inn

By Suellen Alfred

Tom Draper moved from New Jersey to Knoxville, Tennessee, to join his wife, a Knoxville native. Tom adjusted easily to living in Knoxville, but he often had difficulty with the distinct Tennessee accent of some folks who usually lived way out in the country. Well, one day, the lawyer for whom Tom worked asked him to go with him to Crossville up on the Plateau to audio-record a deposition for a case that involved some true rednecks. The recording session went very smoothly.

When Tom got back to Knoxville, he took the recording home in order to transcribe the deposition. He managed the language pretty well until he got to a phrase that sounded like "Hoopin Pine Inn." No matter how many times he listened to the recording, he could not understand the phrase that sounded like "Hoopin Pine Inn." He asked his wife if she had ever heard of a lodging establishment in Crossville called Hoopin' Pine Inn. She was not at all familiar with such a place. A reference to an inn didn't seem to belong in that part of the deposition, but for the life of this New Jersey boy, he could not understand what the witness was saying. Finally, he asked his wife to listen to that section hoping that she could make sense of it she listened, a smile grew wide on her face, and she began to laugh. She told her husband that the speaker did not say "Hooping Pine Inn." Instead, he said "whup your hind end."

It pays to have experts around when you need them.

Teaching Across the Pond

By Suzanne Russell

In 1966, after teaching for five years in Tennessee, I was fortunate to be accepted to teach for DODDSEUR, the Department of Defense Dependent Schools Europe, in other words, schools on United States military bases in Europe. My first assignment was on an Army base in Germany. It had been a German base during World War II, but most of the buildings had survived. One large building had been converted into the American school, but the entire first grade was housed in a separate two-story building with a large, open attic under a steep roof. It was in that attic that another teacher and I were in charge of thirty first-graders. The diversity of the children was an eye-opener and a welcome experience for me, a teacher who had previously only taught white students in segregated schools. Not only did we have black children and white children, but we also had children of other nationalities whose military fathers had married women from those nations. These children were all delightful. They were a joy to work with, except for one little boy, Benjii. His Filipino GI father and mother, with whom I'd had several conferences, both agreed that Benjii was a very angry little boy who liked to bully other children, but they were having no success in changing that behavior. One day he jumped on another student and began hitting the little boy. I grabbed him up and moved him away while Sharon, my co-teacher, comforted the beaten child. I began talking to Benjii in a quiet voice, trying to calm him down. That tactic usually worked, as long as I didn't touch him, but not this time. He glared at me in silence, turned, picked up a desk, and threw it at me! He missed. I called his mother who took him home. He was back the next day, and I watched him more closely so that if I saw a fight brewing, I could distract him with an activity. By the end of the year Benjii and I got along rather well. I often wonder what became of Benjii.

My next assignment was second grade at High Wycombe Air Force Base in England. The school was small, with only one class for each grade. All of the children lived off base. We had no cafeteria, so the children brought their lunches and ate in the library under the watchful eye of the school secretary who was the mother of one of my students, Emily. Emily is forever enshrined in my mind and heart for the essay she wrote confusing two famous Presidents, Washington and Lincoln. She wrote, "George Washington was the first man known to be President. He was President when the Silver Whore was goin'." Emily's mother and I had many laughs over the newly created name for the Civil War!

That same year, Beth, a very bright, well-behaved, daughter of an officer asked to go to the bathroom and I let her go. When she didn't come back after a few minutes I went to check on her. I found her standing in front of a sink where she was holding the head of a first-grader under the water! After rescuing the younger girl, making sure she was ok, and taking her back to her teacher, I reported the incident to the principal who told me he would handle it. I never knew what had precipitated the event and I never heard anything else about it, but I never let Beth go to the bathroom alone again.

The Air Force had assigned a sergeant to the High Wycombe school to handle supplies, transportation, and anything else that needed attending to. Sergeant Chuck was always very pleasant and helpful. Many mornings when I entered my classroom he would have left a funny welcome message on my chalkboard. One said, "Fun lives in the hearts of children; the Shadow knows. Hee. Hee."

At the end of the school year all the teachers had to account for all the items on Chuck's inventory before we could check out. My first year there I could not account for a playground ball, the big blow-up kind. I kept telling him that I had no idea where it was, but he kept insisting that I tell him what happened to it. Frustrated and ready to get out of there, I said, "One day on the playground I saw a child pick up a sharp rock and poke holes in the ball, flattening it. When we went back inside, the child took it with her into the bathroom and flushed it down the toilet." As I talked, Chuck made notes on his inventory form. Then he smiled at me and signed me out! I had no trouble checking out the next year.

From England, I transferred to the Navy base at Rota, Spain, where I was assigned to third grade. The building was typical of any school you would see in the US: two stories, a playground, and a cafeteria. My classroom, however, was very small, and it was located in another building next to the administrative offices. I had seventeen students, and it was apparent on the first class day that all of them were what we now refer to as special needs students. There was no inclusion program at this base. Before being assigned to overseas posts, military families were always asked if they had children with "problems." Because there were no programs for special needs children in overseas schools, those families were not assigned to bases outside the US. Because they needed an overseas assignment to further their careers, many career minded soldiers, sailors, and airmen who were parents of special needs children said their children did not have any problems. As a result, we teachers often found it necessary to develop different assignments for children who were not able to do the work designed for children without special needs. Fortunately, the military now provides special classes and services for children with special needs or mental health problems. A number of my students would have benefitted from both.

I did my best to individualize my students' learning and make the classroom comfortable and fun. One memorable student was Anna, a very unhappy little girl. She was also a kleptomaniac who pocketed everything from pencils to money. The school did have a psychologist who worked with Anna, but nothing changed her thievery. She told me once that her father said they would be going back to the States soon and she could go to a REAL school. I guess he was as unhappy as Anna was. Teaching in that environment was a challenge.

One day a new student came to the class. Her family had just been transferred to the base, and she was assigned to my class full of special needs children because the other two third grade classrooms were overflowing with thirty plus students each. Sara was a bright, socially adept, happy child. Within a week her parents asked to visit the classroom while the children were there. It did not take them long to realize that Sara was much more advanced than the students in the class. After that visit, they requested a parent-teacher conference. At the conference, I explained my teaching method of individualization, but they were not happy. When they asked me point blank if Sara belonged in my class, I had to say no. I thought she would have done better in a room of children who were average to above average in their ability. They thanked me for my honesty, and the next day Sara was placed in one of the other classes.

The following year after one of the other third grade teachers left, I was assigned to her classroom. It was a surprise because I had expected to follow my small group into fourth grade and would have been happy to do so. My new class was large, bright, and full of life. It was a happy, productive year. My most memorable student that year was Kenny who was a real rascal, making jokes, playing tricks, and having a good time, all the while making straight A's. The kids loved him, and so did I. When his shenanigans began to get out of control, I called a parent- teacher conference. We agreed that if he couldn't control his behavior he would be sent home for the rest of the day. That worked for a while because Kenny really loved being at school. The day soon arrived when he just couldn't hold it together any longer, and I had to call his mother to come take him home, which she did. The family lived in nearby base housing; so, it was not long before Kenny reappeared---outside the school windows, dancing, waving, and laughing, getting the attention of everyone inside. The principal was furious! He called Kenny's father who promptly retrieved his son. I am not sure what the father and the principal said or did to Kenny, but when he came back to class, after a few days at home, Kenny was very subdued. It took him only a few days to return to his happy fun-loving self, but he never again crossed over that line into uncontrollable behaviors. I'm not sure if any of the adults handled the situation well. Was I too lenient early on in the school year? Were his parents too lenient at home? Looking back on it, I think Kenny belonged in a gifted student class, but there was no such option in the military schools of that era. Fortunately, there are now.

After Spain, I transferred to Belgium where I taught in the American school at S. H. A. P. E. (Supreme Headquarters Allied Powers Europe, the military arm of NATO which was, and still is, located in Brussels). In addition to the American school, the base housed a British school, a Canadian school, and a French speaking school, all linked by hallways and a common teachers' lounge. All of the children who were not American, British, or Canadian went to the French school, but many of their parents wanted them to attend one of the English speaking schools, and we did take them if there was room. Most of the non-English speaking children in our school were Turkish or Italian, and I always had several of them in my class. There were no classes for English as a Second Language (ESL), so we, teachers and students, got along as best we could. By the end of the first six weeks the children were all speaking acceptable English! I think we call that immersion now!

The next year I was assigned to a first grade class. That was the year of Jeff! I knew Jeff, as did all the teachers, because his French Kindergarten shared the playground with us. Jeff was a loud, badly behaved bully who ignored the rules and the adults who tried to control his behavior. I had several conferences with his parents and the principal, but nothing worked. Finally, the principal had had enough. He decided that Jeff needed to feel the paddle and that I should wield it! He called the father, Jeff, and me to his office, asked me to paddle the boy in front of his father. After that Jeff became a bright, happy, well-behaved student---in my or the principal's presence; but I was told that if neither of us were on the playground or in the cafeteria when Jeff was there, he reverted to his awful behavior. Thank goodness his father was transferred out after that school year.

The next year another child, the direct opposite of Jeff, touched my heart. Amy was a shy, quiet, little girl who needed lots of TLC. One day, as we waited outside for her mother to pick her up, Amy looked up at me with her sad eyes and asked, "Are you happy of me?" Smiling, and trying not to tear up, I replied, "I am soooooooo happy of you! "I had come to realize over the years that if the military families were glad to be where they were, their children were happy, or at least content, and did well in school. If the parents were not happy, it showed in their children. My guess is that such a reality goes for all families everywhere, military or not.

After Spain, I transferred back to England, this time at Upper Helford Air Force Base near Oxford. I was assigned to Kindergarten which has always been my favorite class to teach. The school was a sprawling series of old military barracks linked together by covered walkways. Each barrack was a single classroom, so I had plenty of room for tables, chairs, and activity centers. My most memorable event in that building was the morning I walked in before the children arrived and turned on the overhead lights. There was a spark from one light; then flames began moving through the acoustical ceiling tiles. Luckily, all the classrooms had telephones that were linked to the office. I called and then watched the flames slowly die out just as I heard the sirens. The firemen were fast and efficient. They removed the light and had everything checked and double checked in a matter of minutes, so I was able to have a normal class that day. The children didn't even know what had happened.

After that year, our whole school was moved to a new complex at Croughton, a nearby base. There were two brand new school buildings at Croughton: a high school, and an elementary school. My furniture and supplies had been moved to my new classroom over the summer. There was only one classroom for each grade in the elementary school, and my kindergarteners were only there for a half day. I had two classes each day. The morning class was bussed home after three hours. I had a thirty-minute lunch break, after which the afternoon class arrived.

Kindergarteners are wonderful! At the beginning of the year, I always had a few weepy kids and even more weepy moms! It took the moms far more time to adjust than it did the kids!

My most memorable student was a little boy named Duane. Duane was a very quiet child who loved jigsaw puzzles. In fact, they were his lifeline in this new world of school. It was very difficult to steer him to other activities. When I suggested a different activity center, he would just smile at me and pick up another puzzle. But he came alive when we visited the high school gym. The physical education teacher invited my classes over whenever she could. The gym was full of things to throw and things to climb and bounce on, and Duane threw and climbed and bounced. We always hated to leave.

Croughton was to be my last assignment. After twelve wonderful years, it was time to go home. My family was expanding with new nieces and nephews and my mother was growing older. As I prepared to leave, I remembered an incident from my arrival in Germany. Along with other new teachers, I was waiting in line to obtain a pass for a bus that would take us to our first base. When it was my turn to get the pass, I asked the sergeant behind the desk a question. I don't remember my question, but I certainly remember his response. He looked at me with a sneer and said, "You're a teacher aintcha?" When I responded that I was, he said, "I ain't never learned nothing from no teacher!" His grammar was a good indication that he was right.

When I first began teaching at schools on United States military bases in Europe, I wondered at the time what I had gotten myself into, but after twelve years I knew. I had worked with many delightful children and their families, made many friends and many happy memories.

Thank you For Shopping at Wal-Mart

By Suellen Alfred

"You were one of my favorite teachers when I was in high school. You really helped me a lot." From time to time practically every decent high school teacher in the land has heard some version of that statement from a former student. Hearing such positive reinforcement is one of the many advantages of teaching. A few teachers, however, have heard otherwise.

In the summer of 1990, I went with a friend to Wal-Mart to buy things for my new apartment in Cookeville, where I was moving to take an assistant professor position at Tennessee Technological University. When we got to the checkout counter, a round, short young woman looked at me with a distasteful expression on her face. She went into auto pilot as she began to ring up the items I had brought to the checkout counter. As she was punching in the prices of my items, she curled her lip as if she had just caught the scent of a very foul odor.

As she continued to operate the cash register, she said, "Didn't you used to teach at Walter State [Community College]?" Her teeth remained locked while she spoke – as if she were afraid to open her mouth in a distasteful situation.

"Yes, I did," I said.

Still punching the last several prices, she began to finish ringing up the purchases. All the while, she looked at me with great disgust. Then, she tore the tape from the cash register. As she handed the tape to me, she rolled her eyes, and, all in one swoop, she said, "I think I had you as a teacher. I don't think I liked you very much. Thank you for shopping at Wal-Mart."

We managed to make it to the parking lot without laughing in the poor woman's face. When we got there, we collapsed in hysterics.

Attack

By Heather Gothard

The University of Chattanooga, now the University of Tennessee at Chattanooga, was not so sprawling in the late 60s as it has now become, but it was big enough. Even then, the University was experiencing growing pains and had found buildings and parking lots in make-do locations as close to the main campus as was possible.

Halfway through my Bachelor of Science degree in early childhood, in 1967, I married and was employed as a teacher on a temporary certificate. Exploring my new status as a wife and teacher necessitated a change at UC from full time student to part time evening student. Before the days of backpacks, I clutched my pile of early childhood books, notebooks, and supplies (which collectively weighed at least a ton) in my arms as I headed down the steep hill on then-Baldwin Street beside Hunter Hall. Class was over; day had turned to night. I waited to cross the busy four-lane, one-way McCallie Avenue which was the perimeter of the main campus, and darted when I saw my chance. I was fortunate to have found a parking space in a lot between McCallie and Eighth Street behind a church that had graciously allowed student parking. Street lighting stopped at McCallie, and the fringe area quickly became an inner-city residential neighborhood with small houses and narrow streets.

I walked half a block down McCallie Avenue and turned beside the church through a large archway leading into the parking lot. The stone arch that was so lovely in daylight was spooky in the darkness at night. As I rounded the arch, my jitters were not unfounded as a male figure in a hoodie leaped out and slammed me into the side of the arch. My books went flying, and the fight was on. He pummeled, I pummeled. The fight lasted only moments; adrenaline was high. I lashed out with everybody part that would cooperate: knees, nails, elbows, teeth, feet. Apparently, something connected. The man collapsed onto the asphalt and lay unmoving. My heart hammering, my breath in panting gasps, I grabbed what books I could see and dashed to my car. As I fell into the seat and locked the door, every ounce of that adrenaline oozed out through my toes, pooled at my feet and left me shaking uncontrollably. I glanced up at the arch and could see the dark and still lump that was my attacker. I sat in the car until the shaking diminished and until I felt that I could drive. I pulled out onto the road and knew that I should head for a phone booth and make that call to the police. But I never made the call; I was afraid I had killed the man.

On the twenty-minute drive home, I assessed my condition. I didn't seem to be bleeding anywhere, and nothing felt severely damaged. My appearance, however, was a different story. A glance in the rear-view mirror showed my long hair once piled sixties fashion on my head was now a tangled knot around my ears. I looked like a porcupine with hairpin quills. My blouse was only attached at the waist where it was still tucked into my skirt. I worried that my husband, Terry, would be alarmed when I arrived home. I shouldn't have. I walked into our house and stood there as Terry, sitting on the couch, took stock. Calmly, he said, "How badly did you hurt him?"

For days, I scoured the news for dead men in parking lots and found nothing. So perhaps I didn't kill him after all. If so, I hope he thinks twice about attacking helpless females.

The Umbrella

By Heather Gothard

My husband, Terry, and I recently went to a concert performed by the Nashville Symphony in the outdoor Ascend Amphitheater. Arriving characteristically early, we approached the admission gate as attendants looked through bags and scanned tickets. We were assured of a quick pass as I only carried my raincoat and Terry his umbrella. The day had been stormy with more rain predicted. It was quite a surprise when the attendant informed Terry he could not enter with his umbrella. He would have to leave it outside by a stone wall. No guarantees, she disclaimed, that it would be there when we returned. The umbrella, the attendant informed us, could be used as a weapon.

We located our seats with me grumbling the entire way. How absurd, a weapon! What about metal chair legs and fingernail files and all manner of other potentially dangerous things? I put it behind me, and we settled down to enjoy the concert of John Williams tunes. Somewhere before the intermission, it began to rain, so we draped my raincoat over the two of us as best we could. The hood kept flopping in my face and my knees were getting soaked. As "E. T." finished and intermission began, we agreed we would leave. The concert was incredible, but I was not enjoying the wet yellow flopping hood or my wet and now chilling lower parts. Exiting the gate, we looked to the stone wall in an effort to find Terry's umbrella. The landmark tent he had wisely used to identify his umbrella's placement had been removed, and we now stared at an ocean of umbrellas against the wall. Terry dived in and began his search. I ungraciously mumbled something about just forgetting the blasted thing. He glared at me, shocked. "What? My good Totes?" and went back to the task. Successful at last, we walked to the car and began our journey back to Cookeville.

In the car, I mentally reviewed the events of the evening. When I got to the bit about The Umbrella as a Weapon, my brain latched on it like a snapping turtle. Humph, I thought, reviving my indignation.

Quite suddenly, my body went completely still with an epiphany of a long-ago and mostly-forgotten event: Gail and the umbrella.

At the University of Chattanooga in the mid-1960s, I was pursuing my Bachelor's Degree and lived in a tiny apartment with my roommate, Gail. Gail was a free spirit from Pennsylvania who was in the process of discovering herself away from authoritarian parenting, a process which certainly made for many interesting adventures for both of us. On the day in question, Gail and I needed to walk downtown to pay our rent. The rental agency was an easy walk from the University, and our apartment was located about three-quarters of a mile down McCallie Avenue, a main thoroughfare. As full time students, we continually scrimped to collect the $75. 00 needed for our monthly rent. Gail worked an evening job as a waitress and I had a job on campus as part-time secretary for the music director. With the money carefully tucked into Gail's shoulder bag, we struck out mid-morning between classes for the agency on Cherry Street. The weather was iffy with intermittent bouts of rain, so I carried my umbrella just in case.

We strolled down McCallie chatting about professors, classes, dates (or lack thereof) and other mundane topics. Trouble was the last thing on our minds, but trouble there was just the same. As we neared the Memorial Auditorium, we passed an empty, fenced parking lot. Just past the parking lot gate, we heard running footsteps. With no time for our thoughts to register more than the sound, Gail slammed into me, and a male figure grabbed her purse with such force that it broke the strap on her shoulder. As he zipped past us with her bag, Gail's indomitable I-Am-Woman spirit, my deeply rooted British sense of fair play, and our need to retrieve our rent money fueled the adrenaline necessary for our sprint after the thief. After a short chase, we caught him. In a furious and flailing tangle of bodies, Gail snatched back her purse while I repeatedly bashed the villain with the only weapon I had at hand, my umbrella. Thoroughly umbrella-bashed, the man jerked away, and ran back up McCallie Avenue. We caught our breath and continued on our way to pay the rent. The woman at the Amphitheater was right. An umbrella CAN be used quite effectively as a weapon.

Don't mess with a woman with an umbrella.

Daddy and the Bike

By Joyce Milligan Tatum

My father, Jeff, was a big man who stood a little over six feet tall. He worked at the Ford car dealership in Union City for many years until he was offered a job as a security guard at the Milan Army Arsenal in Milan, Tennessee. With a growing family to provide for, he took the job because, unlike the job as a car repairman, it afforded a steady income. These events occurred during the time of the Korean War in 1949. Because of Daddy's age and the size of his family, he was not allowed to serve in the armed Forces, but now he was proud of his new job because he was working for the United States Army, doing his part for his country.

He reported to his new job on a Monday morning to begin his training. He had a uniform and carried a gun strapped to his side. After two weeks of training, he was given his assignment. He was to report to work on Monday morning, pick up his assigned bicycle, and ride that bicycle around the perimeter of the arsenal to keep intruders out. No one was allowed on the arsenal property without appropriate authority.

As he made his way around the building, he was required to sign a ticket and stamp the time clock to show the time he arrived at a given spot. He had one hour to make it completely around the building and have the tickets stamped. Clearly, this requirement was put in place to show that he was doing his job within the specified time.

Sounds like an easy job, right? Except for the fact that my father had never learned to ride a bicycle! When he got home that Friday afternoon, he told my brothers that they were to teach him "bike riding." Both Jerry and Daniel reluctantly agreed, and so began my Dad's bike-riding exercises. The boys thought it would be easy for Daddy to learn, but they were sadly wrong. My brother Ronnie sat on the porch watching as his big brothers tried for two hours to teach Daddy the art of bike riding.

Daddy would get on the bike with Jerry holding the handle bars and Daniel holding the back fender.

"You can do this," Jerry said. "Just get yourself centered and push off with your right foot and then pedal. It's simple, Daddy."

Daddy ran into the garage door, the side of the house, through my Mother's rose bushes, the garden, and even into the only tree we had in the front yard! He tried his best, but after three days he gave up trying to learn to ride. But he did not give up his job.

On Monday morning when he arrived at work, he had a plan. He picked up his bicycle and went to his starting point. After clocking in, he grabbed his bicycle and ran like crazy pushing the bike to his second stop. Out of breath and panting, he checked in, signed and punched the time clock. It showed that it had taken him thirty minutes to reach the first stop. Daddy knew he had to pick up the pace to stay on time. He began to run again, pushing the bike and made it just in time at the second stop. This continued for hours. At lunch time, his legs were aching so badly he had to lie down on the bench to stretch out the muscles. He never ate his lunch.

After lunch break he continued for four more hours. By the end of the day sweat had soaked through his uniform. When he arrived home, he was so tired all he could do was eat a few bites of dinner and then collapse into bed.

The same thing happened his second day. On the third day, when he got to work, his supervisor was waiting for him.

"Jeffery, you like working here don't you?" he asked.

"Yes sir, I do."

His supervisor waited a few seconds, and then said, "Why didn't you tell me you didn't know how to ride a bike? "Daddy never knew how his supervisor knew about his nonexistent bike-riding skills.

"I tried to learn," Daddy said, "but it's a lot harder than it looks. I figured when you found out I could not ride a bike you would be letting me go. I'll turn in my bike at the guard shack and get my things. Thank you, sir, for the opportunity to work here." And, with that, Daddy turned to leave.

"Wait a minute. You need to turn in your bike and then go see the foreman over on line Z where you can stand still. They have a job waiting for you over there. You won't have to ride a bike anymore or run like a crazy man," the supervisor said, chuckling.

My father worked there until he retired some thirty-two years later. And he never tried to ride a bike again.

Sally, the Mule

By Joyce Milligan Tatum

My father was five years old when his mother died from pneumonia in the early part of the twentieth century. He was one of eight children, the next to the youngest. Molly, the youngest was two years old when their mother died. My grandfather never remarried. He reared his children on his own with the help of the two oldest girls, Effie and Bertha, who were both newlyweds and became more "mother" than sister to the younger children.

My grandfather was a farmer who raised corn, cotton, and cattle. He had a farm out from Trenton, Tennessee in a very rural area of Gibson County. Effie and her husband Russell lived about a mile from my grandfather through the woods. The children wore a path through those woods to Effie's house. Sometimes they would walk, and sometimes the older kids rode Sally, my grandfather's stubborn old mule.

Sally had been in the family for years. She was used first as a plow mule and later to pull the family wagon. Because of her advanced age, she later spent most of her days in the barn yard giving the children rides and munching on apples or sugar cubes they gave her. My father learned to ride Sally in that barnyard.

My father adored his big sister Effie and would often beg his father to allow him to go to Effie's for the day. One early fall day, when Daddy was eight years old, he wanted to visit Effie. He was out of school for four weeks because it was cotton-picking time for the community. Every year the school system scheduled those days as vacation time for students, most of whom lived with families who needed their children's help to pick cotton in the fields. Daddy was too young to keep up in the fields with the other pickers, so he was kept at home doing chores around the house. He had worked quickly that morning, getting all his chores done, and began to beg my grandfather to let him ride Sally to Effie's house for the remainder of the day. Finally, my grandfather granted Daddy's request, provided that he come home well before dark. Daddy set out for

Effie's house allowing Sally to go at a leisurely pace. He spent the day with Effie, helping her with her household chores and working in the flower garden pulling weeds.

Around dusk, Effie told Daddy he better "get on home." Daddy climbed on Sally's back and set off. Now Sally did not like missing meals. She had a sixth sense about her. She realized that with darkness setting in, she might miss suppertime in the barnyard; so she started to hurry along with my father attempting to slow her down. The more he tried, the faster she went. Finally, she had had enough of this little boy trying to slow her down. She kicked up her heels, threw my father off, and ran home, leaving Daddy flat on the ground with an injured ego. Daddy had to walk home alone. He began to cry, knowing he would be in trouble. Sure enough, Sally arrived home and stood at the gate waiting to get in. My grandfather and his oldest son, Bob, came out of the barn and saw Sally without my father. Bob let her in the barnyard where she promptly went to the feeding trough, and my grandfather set out looking for his youngest son. He found him about a quarter of a mile from the house, dirty and crying, under a large willow tree. Grandfather brought him home, cleaned him up, fed him his dinner and put him to bed. Daddy never rode Sally again.

Henry the Rooster

By Freeman Smith as told to Joyce Milligan Tatum

Henry's story began as a blue Easter chick for my son Joey back in 1974. Henry was one of two chicks that year. The other chicken was dyed pink, so we called her Henrietta. As they blossomed and the dye faded, we discovered that Henrietta was also a Henry, so we had Henry One and Henry Two. They turned out to be white leghorn roosters. They grew up to be rather mild mannered roosters until Henry Two passed away. I don't know what it was. Grief, maybe; but after Henry Two died, Henry One became a very big and very mean chicken who never really realized he was a chicken.

Even though Henry was Joey's chicken, Henry disliked Joey a lot. I guess you could say that chicken hated him. Every afternoon, Henry would wait for the school bus to come; and as soon as Joey got off the bus, Henry would attack him – peck at his feet, fly at him, and scare poor Joey half to death. It got to the point where an adult would have to meet the bus every day to protect Joey from Henry's attacks. Finally, I solved the problem. I cut a long piece of cane one day, and from then on, whenever we would meet Joey at the bus, we would have that cane with us to swat at Henry's legs. Not enough to break his legs, but enough to let Henry know he was doing wrong.

Henry loved Nerf footballs. Never saw another chicken in my life that would "make out" with a Nerf football. That chicken would embarrass me to death acting that way, especially when company would come to visit. So when company came, we put Henry in the chicken coop with the other chickens. He wanted nothing to do with those hens and would do his best to get out.

For some reason or another, Henry took up with me. When he was out of the chicken coop, he followed me everywhere I went on the farm. Back behind the shed, I had an electric fence that went around the field where I kept the cows. One morning I headed out to that field to check on my cows. I grabbed the top wires of my fence with my gloves, and climbed over it. That's when I saw Henry headed my way. I figured he would stop at the fence, but that rooster went under that bottom live wire. As he staggered toward me, he squawked the loudest sound I have ever heard coming from a chicken. To a human, that electric jolt isn't much at all, but to a chicken it had to have hurt. I knew I had to teach Henry to avoid the fence. I climbed back over the fence, and here came Henry. I repeated the crossing of that fence two more times with Henry doing the same thing every time, squawking for all he was worth. He never learned. I guess Henry wasn't as smart as I thought he was.

Henry loved to ride in my truck. If I didn't keep my truck windows closed, Henry would be up there doing his business. The smell never bothered me, so I would often leave it there. He would roost on my steering wheel at night. It got to where nobody wanted to ride with me in that truck because of the smell. No matter how many times I kept the windows closed, Henry managed to get in that truck more times that I can count.

And he wasn't too particular about the kind of vehicle he blessed with his presence. One time a salesman from New Jersey came to the house wanting me to lease a section of my land to his company so they could look for oil. I knew there wasn't any oil there, but they were willing to pay me good money, so I agreed to lease the land. The salesman came back to the house a few days later for me to sign the papers. It was a hot day, and I didn't notice that he had rolled down his car windows before he came in the house. He was at the house maybe fifteen minutes. During that time, we completed all the paper work and he then left. A few minutes later he knocked on the door. He was not a happy man. It seems that Henry liked the salesman's car so much, he had flown in through the open window and pooped all over the interior. The salesman could not persuade him to leave. When I went outside, there sat Henry on the steering wheel. I told Henry to get out of there. Sure enough, he got out and strutted away. That salesman never came to the house again.

Later that year Henry met his match. My brother-in-law was always bragging about this little chicken that could beat up any chicken in the neighborhood. Henry was a big chicken; and one day I told my brother-in-law, "I think Henry can take on that chicken of yours. A few days later I told Henry to get in the truck, and he jumped right in. We went to the home of my brother- in-law. Henry immediately jumped out of the truck and went after that chicken. They squawked and fussed at each other so loud you could have heard it over in the next county. Feathers were flying everywhere. In a few minutes, I saw that Henry was losing pretty bad; so, I went over to him, scooped him up, and went on home. I tended his wounds, and we never talked about it again.

One day Henry got in one of the sheriff's deputy's cars. I used to be a deputy and I still had a lot of friends in the department. They used to come by the house to see me and visit. I told Henry to get out of the car and he refused to. He got in the back window and I warned him to get out or else he'd be going for a ride. Last I saw of Henry, he was heading down Highway 70 in the back of the patrol car. The deputy told me that Henry finally got out about 15 miles from the house, but he never showed up again.

I kind of miss that chicken.

Fumigation

By Diane Kostal Dodson

In 1945, Oak Ridge, Tennessee, was the home of men and women who worked on preparing uranium for the atomic bomb. At that time, all the residents in Oak Ridge rented houses from a company that had a contract with the Department of Defense to build and maintain them. My parents and I lived in one of those houses during World War II. When we moved in, we found that the house was full of bugs. The company wanted to spray our house to get rid of them, so they instructed us to leave for the weekend while they took care of the problem. We went to my grandparents' house in Morristown, Tennessee, and returned to Oak Ridge on a Sunday evening. My dad dropped us off at the house so he could go to the store to buy a few groceries. Before we left for Morristown, Mother had prepared a roast and had put it in the refrigerator, so we knew we would have supper when Dad got home from the store.

We found a note on the refrigerator stating that the house had been fumigated and that everything in the refrigerator was okay to eat and drink. My brother Anthony and I asked Mom for a drink of juice. Mom found the open can of Hi C orange juice in the fridge and poured each one of us a glass.

After Anthony took a sip of the juice, he said it did not taste good. He poured most of his juice in the sink and diluted the rest with water from the tap, hoping to improve the taste. Mom smelled the juice and said it was okay, so I took my glass of juice into the living room and drank it. Not long after drinking the juice, I soon passed out on the floor. Mom told me later that when she came in the room and found me unconscious on the floor, I was turning blue. Apparently, whatever the workers used to fumigate the house had seeped into the refrigerator and contaminated the juice, even though the door was shut.

Since Dad had the car at the grocery store, Anthony ran across the street to a neighbor's house and asked them to take us to the hospital. At the hospital, the doctors and nurses worked on both of us.

Although Anthony had diluted the little bit of the juice he drank, he vomited when we got to the emergency room. The doctors pumped my stomach, gave Anthony and me blood transfusions and put us in oxygen tents. I am sure that was the longest day of my mother's life.

While we were at the hospital, my dad returned from the store to find no one home. We had a cat who fortunately had been outside when the fumigation took place. When Dad got home, she followed him into the house and began her usual routine of begging for a snack; so Dad took a piece of roast out of the refrigerator and gave it to her. Fortunately, she immediately threw up and seemed to suffer no other ill effects from her contaminated snack. About that time, a neighbor came over to the house and told my dad what had occurred. Of course, he rushed to the hospital where he was told we were suffering from cyanide[3] poisoning. He immediately agreed to give blood for my brother and me. At the same time, my mom tripped over a cord in the hospital room and suffered a cut on her eyebrow when she fell. So, now, all four of us were in the hospital !!! Two from poisoning, one for an injury, and one to give blood. Fortunately, we all recovered and went home healthy. In a way, getting sick from the orange juice saved our lives. If we had not suffered a bad reaction from the juice, we would have eaten the roast for dinner and perished. You may be sure that when we got back home, we threw everything from that refrigerator into the trash.

Many years later, when I was in nursing school, I discovered that one of my instructors had been working in the emergency room the night that my family came in. She remembered hearing the doctors say that we were suffering from cyanide poisoning! Apparently, that was what the fumigators used to kill the bugs in our house.) She heard one doctor say, "Those children will probably not survive!"

We did survive, and I am happy I lived long enough to share this story!

[3] For some people, cyanide has an odor of bitter almonds, but not every person is able to detect that odor.

Baby Snooks, I Love You!

By Sandra Plant

My younger brother Jim Boy and I grew up listening to radio shows. Our family didn't even have a TV until 1953, but we didn't care. We loved our radio shows. We would sit cross-legged on the rug in front of the big, wooden Philco radio set, eyes wide as we waited for Sky King and his niece Penny to spot a gang of rustlers as Sky masterfully piloted his low-flying Cessna over his Arizona ranch.

And sometimes I almost wet my pants rather than leave at the exciting part when Sergeant Preston of the Yukon was close to saving the lives of two gold miners stranded in a fierce Arctic blizzard. I could just see the dog sled swishing over deep snow, led by the sergeant's faithful malamute Yukon King. At the sergeant's sharp command, "On you huskies!" we knew that lives would be saved and this hearty member of the Royal Canadian Mounted Police would win again.

Of all the radio shows we listened to and enjoyed, none was more beloved than Baby Snooks. The two of us could hardly wait for Sunday night at 6:30 p.m. when the Baby Snooks show came on the air. In a live performance each week, Baby Snooks was portrayed by famed actress Fannie Brice imitating the voice of a mischievous little girl; but to us she was real. Jim Boy and I would howl with laughter at the way she tricked her parents every week. One time, it was her report card that mysteriously disappeared. Another time she hid a bee's nest in the living room where her mother was having her club meeting.

Baby Snooks didn't like going to the doctor. She was just like us. We never liked going to the doctor, either, because it usually meant we would get stuck with a needle.

At the doctor's office, the x-ray machine caught the attention of Baby Snooks.

"Will it take my picture?" she asked.

"Not that kind of picture," Daddy said.

The always curious Baby Snooks began punching buttons on the X-ray machine until it blew up with a loud bang. And Daddy said, "Now you've done it! Promise me that you will apologize to the doctor and explain what happened."

"Oh yes, Daddy, I will." At that point the doctor rushed into the examining room. Seeing the damage, he was irate. "What have you done to my 5,000-dollar X-ray machine?"

Daddy looked at Baby Snooks. Although we couldn't see her, we were sure that our favorite little girl batted her eyes and began her story. "Well, you see, doctor, we waited so long for you that Daddy got mad and kicked your X-ray machine. He's really sorry."

"Get out, get out," screamed the doctor. And Baby Snooks didn't have to go to the doctor after all. Jim Boy and I thought this was hilarious. Why didn't my sweet little brother and I have the nerve to try the tricks that Baby Snooks got by with every Sunday evening?

Sometimes Jim Boy and I would sit in our backyard tree house and talk about things. Sometimes it was parents or friends and sometimes it was the radio shows. One day, my little brother asked me, "Why do you like Baby Snooks so much?"

Being 18 months older and much wiser, I said, "I like her because she is always outsmarting the grownups."

"By being cute," added Jim Boy.

"Why do you like her so much?"

"I like her because she's a little girl about my age," said Jim Boy.

Then came the terrible news one Sunday evening when we took our place in front of the radio. The announcer came on and said, "We regret to inform you that Fannie Brice died today. There will be no more Baby Snooks." We began sobbing so loudly that our Mother came to see what had caused the anguish. "Baby Snooks is dead," I wailed. "The announcer said it on the radio."

Big tears pouring down his pudgy cheeks, Jim Boy sobbed. "The man said, 'No more Baby Snooks.' Does that mean forever?"

Then Mother knelt beside us on the rug, a comforting arm around each of us. She gently explained that Baby Snooks was not a real person. She was performed by an actress, a grown-up lady who pretended to be a little girl. It's Fannie Brice who died, not baby Snooks.

"No, no, she's real," he insisted.

"I thought you knew it was just a comedy show on the radio," Mother said. "I'm so sorry for the bad news."

Later that night, Jim Boy and I lay awake in our twin beds in a cozy blue bedroom. I was trying to work out in my mind how Baby Snooks could be an actress and a little girl at the same time. I heard my little brother sobbing quietly in his bed.

"What is it, Jim Boy? "

"I'm crying because mother said that Baby Snooks is not a real little girl. She's wrong! Baby Snooks **IS** real. And now she's dead." This brought on more sobs. I got up and gave him a Kleenex. He wiped his eyes and blew his nose loudly.

Still sniffling, Jim Boy threw off his blanket and crawled to the foot of his bed where there was a window. Looking out into the night sky with twinkling stars and the sliver of a moon, he whispered his farewell. "Good-bye Baby Snooks. I'll love you forever."

www.ingramcontent.com/pod-product-compliance
Lightning Source LLC
Chambersburg PA
CBHW070451170726
48291CB00005B/1696

* 9 7 8 1 9 4 6 4 7 8 3 4 4 *